CW00822661

Country Moods

Country Moods

Phil Drabble

MICHAEL JOSEPH
London

First published in Great Britain by Michael Joseph Ltd
44 Bedford Square, London WC1
1985

© 1985 by Phil Drabble

All Rights Reserved. No part of this publication
may be reproduced, stored in a retrieval system,
or transmitted in any form or by any means, electronic,
mechanical, photocopying, recording or otherwise,
without the prior permission of the Copyright owner

British Library Cataloguing in Publication Data
Drabble, Phil
Country moods.
1. Zoology——England——Staffordshire
I. Title   II. Birmingham Evening Mail
591.9424'6   QL256
ISBN 0-7181-2590-8

Printed and bound in Great Britain by
Butler & Tanner Ltd, Frome and London

Contents

Acknowledgements

The author and publishers would like to thank the following for permission to reproduce the photographs in this book: the folios refer to the chapters in which they appear.

British Tourist Authority: 61, 64
Derry Brabbs: frontispiece, 63
Cambridge University Collection (copyright reserved): 45
G.L. Carlisle: 11, 58
Bruce Coleman Limited: 33
Farmers Weekly: 29
The Field: 66
Forestry Commission: 38
Fox Photos: 24
David Hosking: 7
Don Hunford: 3
E.A. Janes: 1
Derek Johnson: 6, 21, 26, 40, 49, 57
E. Emrys Jones: 43
Anne Jordan: 27
Maxwell's Photo Agency: 65
John Mennell: 50
Jane Miller: 25
S.C. Porter: 16, 41, 54
Georg Quedens: 9, 14
J. Robinson: 68
Scotsman Features Ltd: 52
John Tarlton: 18, 31, 47 (first photo)
Cdr P.D.V. Weaving, RN: 36
Robin Williams: 22, 47 (second photo), 55
G.K. Yeates: 4

Foreword

This book is compiled from weekly columns which I have been con-
tributing to the *Birmingham Evening Mail* since 1964. The *Birmingham
Post* and *Burton Daily Mail* now take them as well. The articles first
appeared in these papers between March 1982 and November 1984.

Part of the pleasure of writing a regular column for so long is that
it is possible to ride occasional hobbyhorses and spur them into action
when news items rekindle their topicality.

The cause of badgers, which have been so shamelessly badgered, on
purely circumstantial evidence, by the Ministry of Agriculture, is a
case in point. It is rewarding to discover that even implacable bureaucrats can be forced by public opinion to moderate their destructive
plans.

But the greatest pleasure of all that I get from compiling such books
is that I am anchored to my study chair for hours on end instead of
chasing shadows all over the country for less satisfying reasons.

I do not write all the time I sit in front of my typewriter. The study
window looks out over the wood my wife and I have managed as a
wildlife reserve for more than twenty years, and my narrow desk was
specially designed to be so close to the window that it gave truly
panoramic views.

I do not see *occasional* deer or birds or badgers, which at best are
only strangers. I see the *same* creatures so often that I can recognise
them individually – and it is so much easier to write with affection
about personal friends than about casual strangers. And a great privilege to share such friendships with unseen and unknown readers.

P.D.

1. Talent Spotters at the Herons' Ball

Herons look such ungainly birds on the ground, and so magnificent on the wing, that it is easy to assume that they only land to nest, in trees, or to wade in rivers for fish.

At this time of year, early March, our herons spend a great deal of time performing what ornithologists grandly call their courting dance. One after another, they fly down from the wood to settle in a glade in front of my study window. There they sit, looking excessively bored for several hours on end. From time to time another heron flies languidly down, lands at one end of the line and hops, with measured tread, along the line of his (or her) fellows. They take no more notice of each other than a bunch of pimply teenagers, festooned as wallflowers around a village dance hall.

Don't be deceived by that. Human and feathered spectators all have their eye to the main chance. They all assess the 'talent' with expert eyes, however hard they try to look unenthusiastic. When a bird arrives that they fancy, a prospective mate will amble casually after her in a series of gigantic hops that look like a *Sportsnight* replay in slow motion.

Customers at our open air herons' dance hall are less numerous than usual, this year, probably because the hard winter took its toll. They're exceptionally scrawny, scraggy birds, without an ounce of surplus fat, so they can't go for long without food.

When ice freezes the surface of the water, it is impossible for their dagger bills to spear fish beneath the surface. Even in running water, fish grow less active in the cold, and lie quietly at the bottom, too deep for the herons' long bills to spear them. They don't live entirely on fish, though, however loud fishermen complain. Herons catch moles and rats and mice and almost any small creatures that live near the edge of pools and rivers. But, in hard weather, moles hunt deep

1

Patient fisherman. Herons eat rats, moles and other prey as well as fish

underground, and even a skither of snow is a safety blanket that conceals mice and voles.

Now that the snow has gone there are clues of another major item in our herons' diet. Spattered around, without any apparent pattern, I see gobbets of revolting looking jelly. It always appears at this time of the season, but it is only during the last few years that we have known for certain what it is. Our ancestors called it 'star-rot' because they refused to admit that there was anything that they didn't know. So they concocted the most unlikely explanations for phenomena they couldn't explain, which it was difficult for rivals to disprove. They said that if you watched a shooting star flash across the sky, you would see it fizzle out when it burned up. As the tail of the star was extinguished, it spat a mucus gobbet to earth, which was the star-rot that appears in unlikely places every spring.

The real explanation is far more practical. Frogs are spawning in spring and, as everyone knows, each frog produces a mass of frog spawn far bigger than its belly could contain. What actually happens is that the female frog ejects the string of black dots that eventually turn into tadpoles and, as they hit the water, *after* they have been laid, they swell into a mass of jelly that would easily fill a basin. If a heron ate a frog before she had spawned, the eggs inside her would scarcely fill a teaspoon. But, when the herons' digestive juices got to the eggs, they would swell to produce symptoms of acute indigestion!

Instinct came to the rescue. When a heron catches a frog or toad, it does not eat it whole. It dissects it as delicately as a chef carves a joint and, when it comes to the frog's ovary, it does not eat it but plucks it out and drops it on the ground. When the eggs get wet, from rain or dew, they swell into the random blobs of jelly that our grandfathers tried to persuade themselves (and us) were all that was left when a shooting star fizzled out.

Although modern scientists have solved the mystery of the origin of star-rot they are no nearer than their predecessors to solving the mystery of how the heron knows which bits to eat and which to discard.

2. The Tale of the Curate's Dog

When I was growing up, our house was littered with parsons. My father was the vicar's warden so the sitting-room buzzed with parsonic chatter, especially at sherry time. I had such a surfeit of them in school holidays that I have been careful ever since to keep them at a distance, especially as their successors seem such insipid little men by comparison.

Although I was so bored by the sermons of the parsons of my youth, there is no denying that some of them would have stood out as 'characters' in any age. One huge, raw-boned curate looked like an Irishman, had a Welsh name but actually came from Shropshire. He was one of the few I liked. His heart was still in the country, so that he was desperately homesick in our Black Country parish and did all in his power to bring a rural flavour into his life.

The love of his life was a huge chestnut hunter on which he and his father had followed hounds in palmier days and quieter places. It was far from easy to keep this horse in the state to which it was accustomed on the pittance earned by curates in those days, but small things like shortage of cash never daunted him. So it was a common sight, before early morning service, to see the curate, stripped to the waist, scything the churchyard to make hay for his hunter. He kept it on a small-holding between the church and an ironworks, and the cows in the next two stalls also belonged to him. He milked them himself when-ever he could, and the farmer helped out when funerals or weddings conflicted with milking time.

I used to like him because he let me ride his horse. It was a huge, raw-boned creature like its owner, and the ground looked as far away, to a child perched on its back, as the bottom of a chimney to a steeplejack. He once gave me an unintentional fright that was far worse than the temporary terror of tumbling off a horse.

4

We had taken the horse into the country, harnessed to a flat dray that must have given the poor creature an inferiority complex after the top hats and pink coats of the hunting field. It had been a very successful expedition because we had returned with a load of sweet hay donated as a tangible thanksgiving by a grateful farmer. We went into his lodgings to celebrate over a cup of tea, and he told me stories of his favourite dog, which had been his faithful companion for ten or fifteen years. It had been the perfect assistant when ferreting for rabbits and the champion ratter for miles around.

When I asked him what it had been like he opened a cupboard door and there on a plaque, mounted like a fox's mask, was the stuffed head of his inseparable companion. It came as a nasty shock, and I still dream sometimes about the glassy-eyed dog of that curate, and I try to puzzle my mind to analyse his reasons for not burying it decently as most of us would. The answer, I think, was that he was so wedded to the countryside that the noise and bustle and petty wrangling and gossip of a Black Country parish would have driven him mad without his memories of quieter places and simpler ways. So he surrounded himself with rural relics.

The poor chap did have a lot to put up with. He reckoned to visit every parishioner at least once every year – and they did not all have 'Welcome' on their mats. Some pretended to be out and refused to open the door and one hard-faced old hag greeted him with the words, 'If it's religion you'm after, we'm suited,' and slammed the door!

So his horse and his scythe and the sweaty labour of haymaking the hard way, reminded him that heavenly country was not in a different world to the hell of the industrial town that we were still brought up to regard as the 'village'. And after church services were over, he crossed the road to the Queen's Head for a pint with the blacksmith, who still had a forge next door, despite the fact that trams passed between his workplace and the curate's.

To banish him to an industrial parish was like caging a fox, but his horse and his dog's head and his cows made certain that nobody ever imprisoned his mind.

3. Stop the Slaughter of Innocent Badgers*

Healthy badgers in a nature reserve run by the Royal Society for the Protection of Birds may be put in peril because TB has been reported in cattle near Leek in Staffordshire. When Bovine TB broke out in cattle in the West Country, Ministry vets were unable to locate the cause and eventually decided, on purely circumstantial evidence, that badgers were responsible. The result has been that they have squandered £1,000,000 and gassed an estimated 15,000 badgers – but the disease is still spreading.

This gassing caused so much public opposition that the Ministry has been forced to adopt a more responsible and slightly less callous policy. Peter Walker, the then Minister, had to commission an independent report from seventy-six-year-old Lord Zuckerman, who had been a prominent scientist in his day specialising in the anatomy and behaviour of apes. He was well known as an astute politician but he appears to have had little experience with wild badgers. The Zuckerman Report was regarded by some as a whitewash job and it drew criticism from distinguished scientific bodies, including the Mammal Society, World Wildlife Fund, Institute of Terrestrial Ecology, Nature Conservancy Council and the Cardiothoracic Institute. It is now agreed that the cure prescribed by the Ministry is not working and cannot work for a very simple reason.

When a large number of badgers is exterminated in any area there are always a few survivors in crannies that the gas cannot reach or in holes that the Ministry rat catchers did not find. Badgers from the surroundings soon discover that there is a large area of attractive habitat vacant so they move in and mix with the survivors, or even catch the disease if there are still infected cattle. So, sooner or later, the Ministry will be forced to find a more effective method.

Meanwhile the public was so incensed by the mass extermination

6

* This article was originally published in April 1982.

This family of badgers are the lucky ones, protected from the Ministry's vandalism in a nature reserve run by the Essex Naturalists' Trust

of badgers in the West Country that they wrote to MPs to press the Ministry to act in a more humane manner. The result has been that the Government now insist that *nobody* may take or kill badgers without 'consulting' the Nature Conservancy Council. This cuts the Ministry's corns, at least in theory, although there is no reason to believe that the Nature Conservancy Council would withhold agreement without very firm grounds. And anyway the Ministry of Agriculture is not obliged to do any more than 'take note' of the Council. But the Council can specify the methods to be used and the number of badgers to be taken or killed and, most important, MPs seeking specific answers to questions are less likely to be fobbed off.

So far no agreement has been granted for the Ministry to take or kill badgers in Staffordshire, but in spite of this the Ministry held a Press conference and announced that it was going to cage-trap about fifty badgers near Leek and take them away and kill them for examination. I was told this would start in April. I pointed out that the cubs would not be weaned by then and so any suckling sow badgers they took would leave orphan cubs to starve. It now says that it will wait till the cubs are above ground but even that does not mean that they will be weaned. According to Dr Ernest Neal, an authority on badgers, they will not be weaned till June.

An unusual aspect of this case is that the area under review includes a Royal Society for the Protection of Birds nature reserve at Coombes Valley, near Leek. The Society has given permission for badgers on the reserve to be fed bait including coloured plastic beads. By examining the badger droppings in the area it should be possible to establish from the presence of coloured beads in the droppings how far the badgers travel and whether they enter land grazed by infected cattle. The RSPB has given *no permission* to take badgers from its land because it shares the doubts about the effectiveness of the Ministry action.

Even if the Ministry gets a Nature Conservancy Council licence to take badgers, the law does not allow it to enter land without the landowner's or tenant's permission. It did not even bother to invite a representative of the RSPB to its Press conference where it announced its intention to take the badgers. But it cannot enter this land without the owner's permission without a control order. This is made under Section Nine of the 1973 Badgers Act by the Ministry of Agriculture and it only takes effect if no 'prayer' against it is laid by a member of the House within three weeks.

So it is to be hoped that public opinion, spearheaded by the RSPB, will be sufficiently roused to bring officials into line and prevent them committing further carnage at the badgers' expense. So far nothing has curbed the Ministry's extermination policy except public pressure threatening loss of votes.

4. The Bug Soc. and Yaffles

About the only things I liked about school, or my school gaffers or school mates, were the brief periods when I was able to escape. As a member of the school Natural History Society, I was occasionally issued with a pass which entitled me to dodge cricket, which I hated, and spend an afternoon in Randan Woods, in Worcestershire, which sprawled a few miles from the school. My school reports often described me as being consistently 'agin' the government' and as a natural rebel. I have to confess that part of the attraction of half a day in the Randans was to buy home-brewed cider from an old lady who lived at a farm there and to find a safe hidey-hole where I could consume the illicit liquor and have a crafty smoke.

Dunderheaded authority, whether at school or in bureaucracy, is not too hard to outwit, so the thrills of beating the system soon wore off and I began to pit my wits against wild quarry, which was far more rewarding. Deep down in most of us, though we may be loth to admit it, is a primitive streak which leads instinctive hunters to their prey. The form it took with me was to discover the secret nests of wily birds or the caterpillars of butterflies and moths which could be reared in my study at school, and would eventually develop into replicas of the beautiful insects which had produced them.

All the motives were wrong for a budding naturalist. Today it would be illegal to collect the birds' eggs that were my pride and joy at school but at least I had a strict code of conduct. Under no circumstances did I ever take more than one egg from a clutch or tell other boys where I had found the nest. The damage I did must have been minimal and I got most of my thrill from the competitive urge to be better at finding nests than the other boys. It was also a form of collector's mania for having possessions my competitors didn't have.

However reprehensible my motives may have been, there is no

9

A green woodpecker, or 'yaffle', at the nest

doubt that membership of the Bug Soc., as the Natural History Society was irreverently known, sowed seeds that have long since outgrown the thrills of taking eggs or collecting butterflies and moths. As a natural loner, I now get my kicks from watching rather than taking.

In a minor way, I have spent years doing what I can to persuade others that it is far more fun to encourage wildlife instead of limiting its chance of survival by nicking birds' eggs or displaying dead butterflies in cabinets. My one regret is that, perhaps because the competitive edge has been blunted, my ability at actually finding nests has slipped more than I care to admit.

The greater spotted woodpecker always nests in our wood so that the novelty of finding his nest has waned, but the green woodpecker, that fills the air with demonic laughter when rain is imminent, is a far less frequent tenant. They are such flamboyant, gaudy birds, with the most delicate, soft green plumage on back and wings, set off by a yellow rump and crimson head, with eyes as light as shimmering pearls. But it isn't the extrovert brilliance of a feathered dandy that delights me so much as the woodpecker's song.

His country name is yaffle, which has nothing to do with his appearance. The yaffle's song consists of peal after peal of high-pitched 'laughter' that puts me in mind of a girl I knew in childhood. She had an irresistible sense of humour and, when anything tickled her fancy, she dissolved into spasms of belly-shaking brays that set everyone in earshot laughing uncontrollably too. Well, our yaffle reminds me of that wench because, for no apparent reason, he makes the wood echo to the sort of contagious merriment that really makes a party zing.

This year we have had two pairs of yaffles screeching around all spring and, right up to March, we heard one regularly. Then all was silence and we thought that they had found a more up-market residence elsewhere. Just to be sure, I spent many hours quietly wandering in search of telltale piles of wood chippings that would be the clue to the recent excavation of a nesting hole in one of our trees. Every time I gave up the search and resigned myself to the fact that they had found (or made) a better 'ole and the wood would resound again to mocking laughter.

The presence of the birds at this time of year meant either that they were a non-breeding pair or, far more likely, that they had bred and we hadn't found them. Long periods of silence were the clue that the hen woodpecker was incubating eggs and the cock was prudently avoiding drawing attention to the fact by keeping his big beak shut.

Last week, when I took the dogs up the wood for an evening stroll, my attention was riveted by the continual high-pitched squealing of young birds for food. The tree was now easy enough to locate by the racket issuing from a nest bored into the heart of the trunk and, within minutes, the parent yaffles confirmed it by coming to feed their young. The nest was within twenty yards of a path I use daily and I hadn't even noticed the new hole. I must be slipping because I would have been drummed out of the Bug Soc. at school for such an elementary failure.

5. Sounds That Fill a Country Silence

Living a mile from the nearest main road, it might seem possible to 'hear' the silence in our wood. The one snag is that it is never really silent.

As I settled to my typewriter by the open window on a fine June morning, the air was filled with the soft calls of affectionate wood pigeons. Farmers and gardeners hate them for the damage they do to crops. I love them because they seduce me into a primitive state of idleness that lies deep in my nature and, I suspect, in theirs. So, in the shady wood, in the heat of summer days, there is always the sonorous song to while away the boring hours that the woodie's mate must sit upon her eggs. It is only part of the song that converts our wood from inanimate trees to a very virile orchestra.

Several octaves below the musical cooing of wood pigeons, there is a soft, continuous hum that ensures the tree tops are never silent. Far from being the romantic song of courting birds, this is the angry hum of myriads of flies. At least, I imagine it is an angry sound because it is impossible to believe that they kick up such a din for any other reason. But these more or less continuous sounds are merely the background to a woodland symphony.

This year, to our delight, the green woodpeckers or yaffles, have nested for the first time for several years, though they are pretty constant visitors.

If the yaffle and the wood pigeons provide the percussion and the background, there is nothing like a blackbird for the melody. Purists wax lyrical about nightingales and other exotic songsters but I know of no bird to equal an English blackbird. He can fill a town or suburban garden with such music that the memory will always be tinged with nostalgia.

So, I spend countless happy hours simply watching and listening in our wood and, in the intervals between the main bursts of sound, the tiny noises surface. Shrews, which are superficially like small mice, are really more nearly related to moles. They have similar pointed snouts and carnivorous teeth, like dogs, instead of teeth designed to gnaw, like rats and other rodents. Although they are so tiny, they are fierce hunters at heart, not only hunting their prey but fighting each other for territory. When birdsong temporarily wanes, and it really is silent, it is possible to hear the high-pitched, miniscule squeaks of challenging shrews in the grass at my feet.

Other, more discordant, sounds filter in from the farmland that surrounds the wood. When my neighbour calls up his cattle for milking, his voice is as loud as a huntsman cheering on his hounds to catch their fox. And, at this time of the year, there is usually the distant metallic whine of forage harvesters collecting grass for silage, which has all but replaced the sweet-smelling hay of my boyhood.

But, when grass harvest is done and cows are milked, the gentle woodland melody will come into its own again.

6. *Tarka, the Rottweiler*

Tick, my beloved old pointer, died a few weeks ago. She had been a faithful companion, as constant as my shadow, for the last twelve years, and I shall never have a more affectionate and intelligent dog.

Belle, my Alsatian, is delightfully kind-natured, but she is an unobtrusive, rather self-effacing bitch, with not half the character of Tick, who never put a foot wrong but always made her presence felt!

I have been closely involved with dogs all my life so we decided to get another in the hopes that she would follow in the old bitch's footsteps. We didn't want another German pointer, because Tick was so good that I am certain I should always have been comparing the newcomer in an unfavourable light. I was determined that, whatever breed I had, the pup must have been selectively bred for work, not simply for the good looks of the show bench, because I prefer brains to beauty in my dogs.

A friend of mind trains the police-dog handlers of a county police force and he suggested I try a Rottweiler, which is a breed extensively used as police dogs by the Germans, who are less fussy about their criminals being arrested by dogs with 'hard' mouths than our force is! He put me in touch with the owner of a stud dog which has had a lot of success at police-dog trialling, and a fortnight ago my wife and I collected a seven-week-old pup which was our pick of an exceptionally strong litter.

Her ancestors were the dogs used by drovers who took bunches of cattle across Europe before the days of trains and cattle trucks. They had to be tough enough to turn a determined bull which did not agree with the drover about where he was destined to go. The drovers were paid off at the city of Rottweil, which was the hub of the cattle-droving trade, and being as tough as their dogs, they invested part of their earnings in a monumental booze-up. They were not

15

Tarka and Belle thoroughly enjoying themselves in a mock fight on the sitting-room carpet!

stupid enough to leave their cash lying around while they were paralytic, though. They took just enough out to throw a party and fastened the rest in a roll which they fixed to the collars of their dogs. Nobody dared try to remove it until the dog's boss got over his hangover and recovered it himself.

My days for enjoying such wild parties are long since gone, but a canine companion, tough enough to make my wishes respected, seemed no bad prospect. So far I have no reason to doubt either the puppy's will or ability in that direction! She should develop into a powerful dog, rather like an old-fashioned bull mastiff used by game-keepers to arrest poachers at the turn of the century.

We call her Tarka because of her blunt muzzle and dense and shiny otterlike black coat, with a few tan markings to give her distinction.

Belle, the Alsatian, is marvellous with her. The pup hangs on to her tail, climbs all over her, pulls at the other end of her bones without complaint. The only thing we have to watch is that, if we reprimand the pup for going too far, the old bitch is offended, thinking it is her we are scolding. They play for hours in the paddock, the old bitch grabbing the whole of the pup's head in her jaws, but never hard enough to hurt her.

I give her a training session every time I feed her, which is four times a day. I reckon never to hit a dog, but forestall bad habits by bribing good ones at feeding times. At nine weeks old, Tarka will come when called and sit on command in the certain knowledge that she'll get a tit-bit.

She comes with me to feed the poultry and I have nipped ideas of chasing hens by the simple expedient of watching carefully for the moment she is going to start, and throwing a handful of wheat around her ears at the psychological moment. The sudden rattle distracts her attention but does not hurt, and by the time she has recovered she has forgotten what she was about to do!

Modern research indicates that puppies learn more and faster between the ages of six and sixteen weeks than for the rest of their lives. I find it a stimulating mental exercise to encourage good behaviour so subtly that puppies never realise they are being trained.

My little bitch is intelligent, tough and pretty headstrong but, if she does not turn out a topper, it will be my fault, not hers!

7. Count Goldfish as Well as Chickens

I had a delightful letter from a lady recently, saying that a fox was visiting her new house 'from 2.30 to 4 a.m.'. 'I can't say every morning but, by accident, I first saw the fox having a drink out of the fishpond,' she continued. She is nothing if not an enthusiast because: 'The next night I sat all night watching for him. He's beautiful, fully grown, and he wandered all round the garden then lay on the lawn for about fifteen minutes, had a drink and went.' She said that she would like to encourage him, if possible, without any harm coming to him. 'We wondered, if we bought rabbit or chicken from the butchers, would it attract him? There is an old shed in the garden. Would he go into it in the winter if we put straw in it for him?' Then she asks for her name not to be mentioned because 'the gentleman next door keeps birds and, about four doors down the road, a gentleman keeps chickens. If we feed the fox and make him welcome, would he try to get at their birds?'

I am sure that Mrs Blank is very wise to remain incognito because the plain fact is that however high the quality of chicken she buys from the butcher, I have no doubt that any virile fox would really prefer his chicken 'on the hoof' – or whatever the avian equivalent might be. So the gentleman's birds would *not* be safe. She said that she would not tell the gentleman next door (or the one four doors down) until she had asked my advice!

Don't tell him, Mrs Blank, don't tell him. And if you didn't live thirty miles or so from me, I am bound to admit that the advice I am going to give you would be different.

Chaps living in the country, as I do, do not welcome many foxes at our fishponds because most of us keep poultry and are keener on encouraging pheasants to visit us than inedible foxes! But I can quite understand the aesthetic pleasure anything as lithe and beautiful as

18

The urban fox ekes out his existence by scavenging – not goldfish this time but the remains of somebody else's dinner!

a healthy fox would give you when you glanced out of your bedroom window in the early morning.

Without wishing to plant any uncharitable thoughts in your head, I should have an occasional roll-call of the fish in your pond because herons and kingfishers and thieving cats are not the only predators on fat and indolent goldfish. Foxes are not bad at nicking them if they are rash enough to rise too slowly for a nocturnal fly, though I suppose they could be replaced as cheaply as chicken from the butcher.

Beauty is in the eye of the beholder and foxes are certainly among our most beautiful wild animals, even through spectacles that are far from rose-tinted. But, if I wanted to attract a fox, I should not dip deeply into my pocket to buy chicken or minced beef. Foxes are practically omnivorous, eating just about anything from live birds to rotten meat. Indeed, they like their meat so 'gamey' that they frequently bury fieldmice and other small animals they catch and dig them up again only when a satisfactorily ripe aroma percolates up through the earth.

That's why urban foxes have taken to scavenging in dustbins, and I know one highly respectable lady, a pillar of the RSPCA, who was very incensed at the treatment her local foxes meted out to her late lamented pet Pekinese. She had buried him reverently in the garden but, when he began to decay, the foxes disinterred him and left the gruesome traces of their midnight feast in the middle of her croquet lawn.

So any household scraps or meat that goes a bit off in thundery weather will delight the fox. They love fish heads but they also like fruit, and Aesop's fable about the fox and the grapes was by no means far-fetched.

The part of Staffordshire where I live is famous for damsons and, when the bitter, belly-aching fruit loses its tartness and ripens, I often find damson stones in our local fox droppings as proof that they not only know what's good but when it is at its best, as Aesop noticed with his fabulous fox and grapes.

Those who love looking at foxes can not only attract them to the garden, but right up to lighted windows, with almost any scraps. But it *is* a wise precaution not to tell the gentleman next door!

8. *Village in Decline*

My ancient cousin, who lives in the uncivilised heart of Wales, phoned during the bitter cold spell we had last winter. 'How are things with you, old man?' he said. 'They're bloody awful with us. I can't get my car out for snowdrifts so I have to walk to the village for groceries. I am now ninety, you know, and it's surprising what a lot of groceries two old people can eat – if you have to carry them home in a carrier bag!'

We're beginning to feel like that in the village where I live. Not just when we are snowed up, either. Our two nearest shopping towns are both six miles away and the buses run to them only once a week on market day. So if you don't own a car, can't catch the weekly bus or cadge a lift in someone else's car, you are, like my ancient cousin, reduced to walking. And six miles carrying an empty carrier bag there and six back with a full one is more than most folk want.

It hasn't mattered so much until this week, because we have two grand grocer's shops, one at each end of the village. Or we had until August Bank Holiday. Now there is only one. We live a mile out of the village and the shop that is left is at the far end. So instead of going a mile each way for a loaf of bread, we shall have to go two each way – four in all.

Our local shop, Jo and Chris, closed down last week and the folk who have bought it want to use it as a house and not a shop. Reg and Pat, who keep the shop at the far end of the village, sell almost everything you can think of, from sherry and frozen chips to peaches and chocolate and thin-sliced bread. But two miles extra on the journey costs a couple of bob in petrol and wear and tear, if we take the car, or half an hour if we walk it.

In the twenty years we have lived in the village a handful of little shops has closed and an old book on Staffordshire, printed in 1851,

21

shows just how serious the decline in the richness of village life has been. There were then 1,508 inhabitants in the village of Abbots Bromley which William White, the author, described as 'a decayed market town' but I don't think he meant to be rude. There was a Post Office where letters were received and despatched 'at 6.30 in the morning and 8.15 at night'. There was then a baker, a nailmaker, a seedsman and carrier, a cooper, a basketmaker, a shopkeeper, a corn miller, a chemist and druggist and a plumber and glazier, who also kept the Post Office. There was a swine dealer and though we can do without one now there was a Revenue Officer. There were also five butchers, two drapers, three blacksmiths and nine boot- and shoe-makers. To cater for their spiritual and carnal needs was an assort-ment of clergy, schoolmasters and seven pubs, five of which still flourish.

The population is now about 500 more than it was in 1851, and to passing visitors the village would not look so very different because the planners have tried to avoid altering houses that front on the village street. They haven't entirely succeeded because a few of the gaps have been filled with structures that look about as much in place as gold teeth in a maiden's jaws. But tucked away behind the original houses there is plenty of evidence of the work of speculative builders with their mass-produced dwellings as indistinguishable from each other as the 'little boxes' in the popular song.

Many of the folk who live there seem to me to have chosen the worst of both worlds, town and country. They have up to thirty miles to commute to work, and when they get home they have no more privacy than in modern estates in the suburbs where at least they don't have the daily hassle of commuting.

Where I live, a mile out of the village, nobody delivers anything. The milkman leaves our milk three times a week at the butcher's, a neighbour kindly fetches the letters and papers, and we keep our bread in the deep freeze, replenishing supplies on weekly shopping trips to town. The snag is that we keep forgetting things, and now that Jo and Chris have gone the price of a bad memory is an extra couple of miles' trek to the nearest grocer.

9. Poison in the Mud

You may not have heard of Dr Greg Mudge and I confess that the name was new to me until last week. He has been doing some sophisticated detective work to uncover the villain who has been laying low a lot of wildfowl.

With thousands of sportsmen going duck shooting every week in the shooting season, it may come as no surprise that the lives of about a fifth of the 2,500 mallard duck he examined were threatened by lead shot. The surprising thing about Dr Mudge's findings is that it wasn't the lead shot fired at them from shotguns that put them in peril of a premature end. It was the lead shot that they had eaten.

Birds that eat grain as a major item of their diet do not chew it up, as we would. They have no teeth. What they have, deep down in their insides, is a miniature corn mill, which can grind grain and the shells of snails and the scaly coverings of the insects they eat finely enough for digestion. This is done in a gizzard, which uses small stones and bits of grit and immensely powerful muscles to grind the relatively soft grain against much harder grit and stone.

Duck are designed to dibble about underwater where the mud is so thick that it is often impossible for them to see what they are collecting in their wide, flat bills. When they feel something hard, they swallow it down, in the belief that it is either edible grain or insects, or even harder stone or rock chippings, which will be useful to grind the edible particles they dredge up. It never occurs to them, of course, that some of the hard bits they feel between their flat bills are neither food nor the hard material they need to grind it. Their bills were designed before lead shot and, dredged up with thick mud, a lead shot must feel indistinguishable from a useful pebble.

The lead that Dr Mudge has been finding in his dead ducks did not come out of shotgun cartridges which hit the birds but those that

This pair of mallard are extremely healthy – but how long before they suffer through the carelessness of sportsmen?

missed. When a shooter is after duck, the commonest way of outwitting them is by flighting. That is to say, the shooter conceals himself near the water's edge and waits for the birds to flight in to feed at dusk or dawn. As the light worsens, the chances of hitting the target also fade so that there are a high proportion of misses. What goes up must come down again, and the spent pellets often come to rest in shallow water and sink into the surface of the mud. The pellets are taken in and, being softer than grit, they are ground up in the gizzard and pass into the system as pure – or impure – lead poisoning.

This shot and the weights that fishermen use on their lines are now among the commonest and most dangerous causes of the deaths of swans and duck and other waterfowl. Dr Mudge found evidence of lead poisoning in mallard and gadwall, greylag geese and pochards, swans and tufted duck, all of which were poisoned by the men who missed their mark.

Wily birds may outwit the men who fire shots at them, simply by being wary enough to spot the hides and keep out of range. But there is no way of avoiding sucking up lead shot along with the normal food they find in mud. It is a problem that grows gradually worse because lead does not disintegrate or corrode so that the number of lead pellets lying at the bottom of muddy pools constantly increases, lengthening the odds on picking them up accidentally. Dr Mudge found up to thirty pellets to the square metre in some of the washes in East Anglia.

The answer is to use steel shot, which would not be poisonous, instead of lead. This is insisted on by law in parts of the United States. Our cartridge makers say it would increase the wear of shotgun barrels, be more expensive and reduce 'killing efficiency'. Another example of the unacceptable face of Big Business, which should bear part of the blame if the anti-sport lobbies grow annually more powerful.

10. Hard Weather Helps Insects

When I heard that 1982 was to be the Year of the Butterfly, I wrote it off as just another non-event. We're always having the Year of this or that, and apart from a few boring do-gooders prattling away at the start of the campaign, that is all we usually hear about it. For years, butterflies have seemed such a lost cause that having a year in their honour seemed more of a requiem mass than any promise for the future. So I promptly forgot all about it.

But the last few weeks of September there is no doubt we have had more butterflies in our wood and garden than I have seen since I was a boy more than half a century ago. We have had a nice few for several years which I confess have made me feel a little smug. I have taken great pride in encouraging wild flowers to grow which have been getting scarce on agricultural land, presumably due to modern farming methods.

Conservationists have been drumming it in for years that agricultural pesticides have been exterminating insect friends as well as foes – and herbicides have been wiping out the food plants that so many insects need. So, when any friends have remarked on the scarcity of colourful butterflies, I have shrugged it off with the remark that greed for the last farthing of profit tempts farmers to slaughter every insect and plant except the species that will send them laughing to the bank. Now I am beginning to wonder.

There can't be much doubt that spewing poisonous chemicals over the land does immense damage to useful insects as well as to pests. Selective herbicides, that kill every 'weed' and leave the crop, must leave myriads of caterpillars to starve, to say nothing of birds that would have fed on the caterpillars. But if you look at the tiny clusters of eggs – no bigger than pin heads – that appear on cabbage leaves, it is quite clear that a hatch of Cabbage White butterflies don't need much of a foothold to mount an invasion.

We don't allow any pesticides or weedkillers in our wood, as the most I ever do is to scythe nettles and thistles that threaten to seed on to our neighbours. So we've always got a nucleus which could start quite a population explosion if ever conditions were suitable.

Most people know about hibernation, when creatures that could not thrive through the winter simply sleep through it. A few animals, like hedgehogs, hibernate largely because there would not be the beetles and worms and slugs they need to feed upon. Some insects lay eggs in spring, which don't hatch out till the weather gets better. Others, like many butterflies and moths, go to sleep in October and November and wake to feed and lay eggs in spring. The critical question is: 'What wakes them up when winter is over?'

Most of them have a mysterious process called the diapause. This is a mechanism which triggers their whole body to change gear from the deep sleep of hibernation to the intense activity necessary to get their digestion and reproductive organs active after many months when, to all intents and purposes, they have been almost dead. Diapause is not triggered off when the weather gets kinder in spring. On the contrary, it is triggered off by exceptionally hard spells. It is one of Nature's wonderful safeguards to prevent hibernating creatures waking up in an exceptional warm spell which might be followed by harsh weather that would immediately sign their death warrant. So Nature has arranged that hibernating creatures don't wake up till winter is past and that is normally after very hard weather. In exceptionally mild winters, the diapause can actually cause scarcity the following year by neglecting to give the signals to renew activity.

Last winter we certainly had such a harsh spell of cold that it actually froze the diesel oil in my tractor and bunged up the central heating. Although this was uncomfortable for us, there is no doubt that it triggered off the diapause in a great many insects that might otherwise never have wakened.

Last week, in late autumn sunshine, we counted more than a hundred butterflies on the sedum and michaelmas daisies in the garden. Red Admirals and Peacocks, Wood Fritillaries and Painted Ladies, as glamorous as their names, gave thanks for the cold snap last year and promised similar compensation if we have another this winter.

11. Late Arrivals Come Off Best

I have found several shells from wood pigeons' eggs lying in the woodland rides this week. They were freshly hatched, for the shells had not been splintered at random as they would if crows or jays or magpies had stolen them. They had been neatly capped, as cleanly as you might decapitate a boiled egg for your breakfast. Picking one up to examine it closely, I could see that the egg had been chipped from the inside by the squab battering its way free to the great unknown.

There is not a shadow of doubt that quite a number of wood pigeon eggs have hatched only this week, in the middle of October. Spring is the traditional time for birds to breed so that, at first sight, young birds hatching now would seem to have a pretty slim chance of survival. These youngsters are different. A wood pigeon nest is just an untidy platform of twigs, precariously balanced in the fork of a tree, in which the bird lays a clutch of only two shiny white eggs. In spring, before the leaves are properly covering the trees, the nest is conspicuous from the ground and the glaringly white eggs are equally conspicuous from above. Stoats and cats see the hen bird sitting on the nest and crows and other robbers see the eggs when the hen gets off to feed.

Probably ninety per cent of the early nests are robbed so that the eggs are little more than a crop of food on which other animals and birds can feed.

Judged by the standards of early broods, wood pigeons ought, in theory, to be rare species instead of agricultural pests. Although they lay only two eggs to a clutch, while blue tits or wrens might be laying ten or twelve, pigeons are more persistent. They lay two, three, or sometimes more, clutches in a year.

Although this clutch is pretty late, the good news is that food is so plentiful that the danger of other birds robbing them is far less than it was in spring. Gone are the days when every pair of jays had a

Wood pigeons do not have many friends in country communities so they
need sharp eyes and every trick of flight to survive

nestful of chicks which they desperately tried to find enough grubs
for. The young jays are fledged on acorns, which are among the
favourite of all foods for the gaudy robbers. Old jays, too, are busy
acorning and I don't suppose that it ever occurs to them to hunt for
pigeon squabs when all respectable pigeons should have stopped
breeding.

The danger of falling prey to other creatures has so diminished
that, even in a wet month like this, the odds stacked against pigeons
rearing a late brood are not nearly so bad as they are in balmy
summer weather. Add to that the fact that, once out of the nest and

safely on the wing, the young birds can stuff themselves with so little effort that they ought to grow like weeds.

Sadly, from the farmers' point of view, these 'afterthought' young will be joined at any time by reinforcements from the Continent, for autumn brings its migrants. Some, like woodcock, are more than welcome, but wood pigeons fall into the class of immigrants that we should prohibit if possible. Cauliflowers, cabbages and other winter greens have already had a good hiding from caterpillars that have thrived in this Year of the Butterfly. Now they are due for a bashing, not only from our bumper crop of late-hatched wood pigeons, but from their immigrant Continental cousins, too.

So pigeon clubs all over the country are oiling their guns and getting out their bundles of camouflage netting and capes bought from government surplus stores. They will set up cunningly concealed 'hides' near vulnerable crops and wait, at dusk, in woodland for the flocks of birds to come in to roost. They will either shoot the young that dodged the jays, and their friends from abroad that are reinforcing them, or plundered crops will rocket the price of winter vegetables even more than usual.

12. When Nature's Clock Stops

A reader from Ombersley, in Worcestershire, sent a pleasant photo-graph of what he described as 'a spring lamb and mum'. He added that there is nothing unusual about it – except that it was taken in September! He thought it was strange because, he said, 'sheep have a programmed reproduction'.

It is normally a programme devised by the farmer. Sheep naturally come into season as the days shorten, about October, and as their gestation lasts five months, they will lamb about March, just as the fresh young grass is springing. Once they come into breeding con-dition, they are ripe for mating every eighteen days so that, if the ram does not tup them first time round, he will have to wait eighteen days and their lamb will be that much younger than lambs from ewes that were ready at the time the ram was introduced.

Nothing in Nature works strictly to programme, and if the ram was run with the flock all the year round, there is no doubt that odd ewes would lamb at all sorts of seasons. Wild animals take instinctive ad-vantage of this type of exception because it may happen that young born at an unusual time find that food or weather is more favourable than at 'normal' times so that the odd man out would grow better than his competitors and would survive to produce exceptional off-spring. That is how evolution has 'improved' species from simple forms of life to advanced (?) animals like Man!

The most likely explanation for the out-of-season lamb is that the ewe conceived in the normal way but aborted, possibly because she was chased by a dog. She would come into season again and the ram would tup her for the second time.

Of course, there is nothing that farmers would like better than sheep that would produce two crops of lambs a year. By careful selective breeding they have got one breed, the Dorset Horn, that can

31

have two crops of lambs in a year, though not regularly. That, from the farmers' point of view, is the good news. The bad news is that Dorset Horns are not very big sheep and their lambs do not grow very fast! Scientists are working on the problem, wondering why it is that the sheep come into breeding condition in late autumn: they gradually isolated the possible causes until they discovered that the shortening days affected hormones that triggered off ewes to come into season. They discovered that if they kept ewes in sheds lit only by artificial light, and gradually reduced the hours the lamps were lit, they could induce the ewes to come into season at unusual times of year. They have actually got as far as getting three crops of lambs from a ewe in two years.

Keeping them indoors with artificial light is so expensive that the extra lambs produced do not pay expenses. I am very glad they don't because I think there are already too many people messing about with Nature and keeping stock in uncomfortable conditions for the last catch-penny profit.

Apart from such gimmicky tricks, sheep farming has pretty sophisticated methods of management. Different farmers want their lambs at varying seasons. Our land is heavy clay, for example, and the flush of spring grass is far later than on lighter, warmer soils. My neighbour likes his lambs ready to go out in the fields about April, when the grass is tender and the ground has dried a little from winter rains and doesn't trample into a quagmire. So he counts five months back from March and introduces his ram to the flock in October. Not all the ewes will be in season and, even if they were, he wouldn't get them all in lamb the first time. But the bulk of his flock, which overwinters in a covered yard, is ready to go out with their lambs on to pastures in optimum condition.

13. High Jinks of the Birds That Stick Together

Having been born in the Black Country, I was practically raised with pigeons. The chaps I grew up with all kept a whippet or bull terrier for a bit of sport on Sundays, and pigeons for Saturday afternoons. Just to top things off, many had roller canaries in the kitchen to enter in singing contests in local boozers. It's not surprising therefore that I've always been a dog man and have kept most sorts of stock as well. I did have some racing pigeons when I was a kid, but pigeon racing is men's work, so I never did any good.

Most Black Countrymen have a flair for stockmanship, but pigeon racing is a thing apart. It is an art, not a science, and the skills of getting birds physically fit enough to fly for hundreds of miles at racing speeds needs a lifetime's experience. The real racing men are so convinced that their birds are so much better than their rivals' that they not only pay to enter their birds in the race but back them heavily to win. I've never been a betting man because it goes against the grain to see cash made the hard way going so easily.

I kept tipplers instead for a while, because, to my mind, the art of tippler flying exceeds all other forms of sport. When you have got a racing pigeon fit, you send him away to the race point, perhaps hundreds of miles away across the Channel. When the race starts and he is liberated, he has to fly home or get lost or drown in the sea. He has no choice. But the thing with tipplers is to persuade the birds to fly as long as possible, in sight of their home loft, just for the joy of it. The tipplers that stay airborne for the longest period win the contest and they are free to pack it in at any time they feel tired. It is a yardstick of the skill of the men who get them physically fit that winning times are often more than fourteen hours' flying for the sheer joy of it, not because they have to!

The greatest enthusiast wouldn't call it a spectacular sport, though.

33

All there is to see is a 'kit' of birds, flying round in circles, often so high that they look no bigger than sparrows, for hour after hour. Tumblers are different. Tumblers fly round in a kit, but every now and again pause in a flight and perform a series of back somersaults. There are various breeds of tumblers from prestigious Birmingham Rollers, which should all roll together as a kit, to rare Oriental Rollers which are individual performers, often flying by themselves and suddenly going into rolls. Nobody knows quite why these pigeons roll. It is an accomplishment that is theoretically self-cancelling because birds which grow too enthusiastic roll so fast and so far that they are unable to check themselves and hit the ground. The deepest rollers of my Orientals all committed suicide by crashing to earth, so that natural selection chooses the survivors as breeding stock. The fittest survive because their parents didn't roll.

Some people say that pigeons roll because they have a brain defect that causes some sort of fit. Others say that it is sheer exuberance. I am certain that it is a conscious act because Birmingham Rollers roll together as a kit and flutter down like falling leaves.

A neighbour of mine is one of the Top Chaps in the pigeon racing world, so I asked him for an introduction to somebody who would sell me a kit of tumblers that would delight my eyes with their aerobatic somersaults to remind me of my childhood in my declining years. That's where I made my mistake, for a little knowledge is a very dangerous thing! I had told my friend that I wanted to see them *tumble*. I should have said *roll*!

There is no end to the variety in colour and size and shape of exhibition pigeons and there are the Rollers, which I wanted, which 'tumble' or turn somersaults in the air. When I was a kid, we always referred to them as Tumblers, so it didn't occur to me to ask my friend for Birmingham Rollers, which is the proper term for what I wanted. In due course he turned up with five pairs of magnificent birds – at a very magnificent price! My instructions were that on no account was I to let them out but to breed youngsters off them and experiment with them rather than risk losing my expensive breeding stock. So I built an aviary and ogled at them through the wire netting.

They were truly beautiful birds, much larger than the common little tumblers of my youth, but I assumed that you get what you pay for and that their size was proportional to their price. They bred quite freely and I got fed up with creeping round to their pen at the back of the tractor shed to admire them. I decided to go mad and gamble that they wouldn't fly away if I let them out. They didn't. It was all the idle toffs could do to fly up and perch in the tops of the nearest trees, where the leaves concealed them so that I couldn't even admire their good looks.

I asked my friend's advice and he said that I had probably got them too fat and lazy in their aviary. So I fed them by spreading their corn over a wide area to make them work for their living. It made very little difference. A couple flew far enough into the open to get knocked-off by a sparrow hawk, and I hope they gave him indigestion. The rest lounged about like fashion models, which was not the object of my exercise! So I got in touch with the chap who bred them and discovered that the whole affair was a misunderstanding. He had gathered that I wanted Tumblers (the term I used in my ignorance) and had sold me a kit of West of England Tumblers, not Birmingham Rollers. They are exhibition birds, which strut about in show rings, not performing birds at all. So now I am starting all over again. I shall try to find someone who will swap my high-priced dandies for a kit of Brummies which will put trapeze artists at the circus to shame by their antics, and I shall get them from someone who shines in the world of competition Rollers. Nothing worthwhile is easy!

14. Ministry Madness*

The Ministry of Agriculture has gone poison mad. Rabies is a killer disease which, since the last war, has been spreading towards our shores at twenty or thirty miles a year, across Europe from Poland. The main agent that is believed to spread it on the Continent is the common red fox. So the Ministry of Agriculture hatched a plot to kill foxes over here whenever the disease arrives. They proposed to distribute 8,000 fowl heads, laced with the deadly poison strychnine, around each spot where the disease is reported. They could scarcely have chosen a poison that is more persistent or a bait that is more universally attractive. Not only will foxes eat fowl heads but so will dogs and cats and most other carnivorous animals and birds. Strychnine is so persistent that it not only kills the animal that first eats it but also anything that eats the victim or the victim's victim. The plan they proposed was so irresponsibly indiscriminate that nobody could say where it would finish, as their poison baits could end by killing all sorts of unintended animals in food chains.

I suggested in *No Badgers in My Wood* that, if the men from the Ministry really thought it essential to kill foxes by poisoning them, the least they could do would be to choose a poison that would soon become harmless if not eaten, and a bait that would be attractive to foxes but not to other animals. The germ warfare men at Porton Down were briefed by the Ministry to devise a poison that was so acute that it would kill victims before they could crawl away to die out of sight and unstable enough to become harmless if not eaten quickly. The Ministry told a national newspaper, in March, that they had done trials of their latest latent brew, in Scotland, during January and February, and that they were 'evaluating' the results.

When no progress was reported after a further six months, I inquired again, first to be told that results were still being evaluated

36

* This article was originally published in November 1982.

The common rabbit is hunted not only by foxes and stoats but also by protected species of birds of prey. The first in a lethal food chain?

and then that they had laid 300 baits and killed nine foxes in three days.

When they didn't like wood pigeons, they laid baits laced with alpha chloralose, which they claimed was 'not a poison but only a narcotic'. An overdose killed them, in spite of the claim, so that the distinction between an overdose of a narcotic and a lethal dose of poison is no more than cynical bureaucratic bumble.

The latest victim is the common rabbit. When I was young, the professions of rat- and rabbit-catchers were respected and skilled. Modern pest officers use gas and poison, which can be administered by any oaf, and the Ministry is considering the destruction of millions of rabbits, which it claims are now a plague, by laying baits of poisoned chopped raw carrot.

Recent experiments in Surrey, claim the Ministry, show that 'nasty' creatures, like rabbits and grey squirrels, eat the carrot, but 'nice' animals, like deer and voles and other wildlife, ignore them. What rubbish! Our deer love carrots and so do lots of birds. And what happens if someone innocently shoots a dying rabbit and sells it for food?

When it took the Ministry seven years to discover that gassing badgers is unacceptable, who will trust them to spew deadly poison over the countryside?

15. *Hedging My Bets with an Expert*

Ten or twelve years ago I planted a hedge all along one edge of my wood, when the fashion was to grub hedges out instead of planting them. I should have liked a blackthorn hedge but the price of young blackthorn plants was several times the price of hawthorn or 'quicks' of similar size. So I settled for one blackthorn to every five quicks.

The reason why I wanted blackthorn was that it increases by sending out suckers from its roots and there was all the room it could need to spread on the wood side. I should have liked a jungle of prickly plants to keep out the trespassers and give perfect sanctuary for birds to nest. A fringe benefit would be the sheaves of white blossom that comes out before the leaves in early spring and sloes, to brew sloe gin, in autumn.

The hedge thrived, except where it was too overshadowed by trees and, to reward my frugal planning, the blackthorn grew even better than the quicks. A couple of weeks ago, the young plants were rising, slim and elegant, to a height of ten or twelve feet. Left to themselves, they would have gone on growing upwards, shading out the hedge bottom till a pony could have walked through it.

The modern way of dealing with hedges that haven't been grubbed out is to trim them with mechanical hedge-cutters worked from a tractor. It produces a horrible, mutilated mass of shattered twigs which are eventually hidden by leaves the following spring. If the process is repeated too often, the hedge grows thinner and more useless at the bottom.

The old-fashioned way of caring for hedges was to cut and lay them. The snag in this is that, unlike trimming from a tractor, it is a very uncomfortable job. Hedges, especially blackthorn hedges, are prickly brutes, designed by nature to seek the most tender parts of human flesh and rip them roughly from the bones. Another

39

disadvantage is that, while most morons could be taught to drive a tractor, proper hedge-laying is a highly-skilled job which takes far longer than thrashing it into shape mechanically; craftsmen who can still do the job are few and far between.

My work gives me the privilege of mixing with all sorts of country-men, especially craftsmen who have inherited the skills of their fore-fathers. I knew that, if I could persuade him to come, Fred Goodall was just the chap I needed. So, a couple of weeks ago, Fred turned up with an axe sharp enough to behead a criminal, a slashing hook to discipline thinner twigs and branches, and a pair of leather gloves that were proof against the most vicious thorns.

The ten-foot plants were about two inches thick at the base and Fred sliced them almost but not quite through a few inches from the ground. An ignorant friend, who called when he was working, thought he was just cutting the hedge down and leaving a mess. He couldn't believe that the tiny sliver of bark and wood that had been left had any chance of survival! When each stem was cut, Fred laid it almost horizontal, along the line of the hedge so that, instead of being ten feet high, it covered a space almost ten feet along the ground. As he worked along the hedge, each cut plant was laid over the next and woven between hedge stakes driven in, to give the effect of a living, plaited hurdle. Finally the top was laced with pliant hazel, to add to the effect of a continuous hurdle, about three feet high, fashioned by an artist.

The blackthorn I planted had already suckered and Fred split off bunches of these suckers from the root stock and replanted them in the gaps where overhanging branches had shaded out original growth. To prevent these new plants being dwarfed, he trimmed off the bottom branches of the trees, to show off their noble trunks and let more light in.

It may take a couple of years for the hedge to recover, but then it will be perfect, a defiant symbol that money and machines don't rule us all.

16. *Art in Concealment*

There's nothing like animals to cut you down to size. I go round our wood at least three times every day I am working at home; I pick a different route through the rides every time and I am as observant as most. So I reckon that I know almost every square yard and blade of grass and the birds and animals that live there. I know what I see and I think I know what I don't see.

The result of this is that I was quite sure that my muntjac deer, Min and Jack, had either wandered away or died, for I had not seen them for three weeks. Then on Saturday morning my wife and I took the dogs out and, standing in a clearing where I have so often seen them before, were Min and Jack, watching our progress from ten yards away.

It was an object lesson about never drawing conclusions that you can't substantiate. By the beginning of December it was obvious that they had finished the acorn crop and other goodies that are part of the autumn harvest, so they had decided to fall back on the flaked maize and wheat I put out for them. It was therefore logical to suppose that we should see them regularly again and that they would call at the house for food as often as the birds do.

Such glib theories are not borne out by fact. I've been round the wood even more often than usual since then, making special journeys at dawn and dusk, just to cover chances that we shouldn't meet up. For all the evidence of their presence, they might as well have vanished into thin air. We haven't seen hair nor hide of them again.

Now, if it is as difficult to see relatively tame, hand-reared animals like our muntjac, I wonder how many really shy creatures like stoats and foxes are there without me knowing? Our wood covers eighty acres and there is the meadow, Daffodil Lawn, at one end, and the paddock and Dunstal Pool by the house, at the opposite end of the wood.

Jack crosses the paddocks in front of the sitting-room window

In order to encourage as wide a variety of wildlife as I can, I deliberately provide a wide variety of cover. There are about forty acres of hardwood, mainly oak and birch and ash and alder, running right up to the house. On the far side of the pool we have made a clearing of sweet grass and clover to provide a 'deer lawn' that will attract the deer to graze where we can watch them through binoculars. Round three sides of this clearing there is a big stand of pine trees planted by the Forestry Commission before we came – two more small pools, and patches of dense bracken and reed and thicket which make ideal nesting cover for birds and sanctuary for deer, foxes and hares to lie-up snug and private.

Our muntjac probably have been feeding so well that they have lazed away the daylight hours in some such thicket ever since the acorns dropped.

It is astonishing how close shy, wild creatures will lie if the cover is good and they do not think that they have been detected. There is a fallen log in Primrose Dell, at the far end of the wood, that always catches the faintest glint of wintery morning sun. I was wandering down there one morning when something as bright as a glistening jewel caught my eye. When I stopped to look directly at it, it immediately melted away. It was an old fox that had been lying on the warm bark, basking in the weak sunlight. His tawny fur blended in with the mossy bark of the tree trunk so that the camouflage was well-nigh perfect. He knew, by instinct, that he was safer from detection lying motionless than if he got up to run away – so he never flinched until I caught his eye. The instant he realised our eyes had met, he simply disappeared, but I have often passed within spitting distance of rabbits and hares that didn't know I'd seen them.

I expect that the muntjac and a lot of other creatures often laugh up their sleeves at the chap who doesn't notice them.

17. *The Goose of Christmas Past*

The chap from whom we have bought our Christmas turkey for years has stopped rearing them. He has decided to buy this season's birds from an intensive turkey farmer and sell them on to his old customers. Not to me he won't. I prefer my birds reared the old-fashioned way, free to run about the paddocks by the farmyard and build up a bit of muscle instead of layers of spongy flab.

It so happens that I was recently lumbered with a professional engagement which involved a pre-Christmas dinner in the sort of flashy hotel where most of the food comes out of a boiler bag. You could almost have wrung the turkey out. Soaked cotton wool would have been tasty by comparison. The stuff that landed on my plate might have been boiled or stewed or steamed but I am pretty sure it had never been roast, as the menu proclaimed.

Anyhow, we're having goose for Christmas, one of our own home-reared birds, and it is already hanging in our cool larder to ripen and mature.

The Black Countrymen of my youth used to say: 'The goose is a very foolish bird; too big for one, not big enough for two.' Well, ours was twelve pounds dressed, so our modern appetites have either declined or our geese are bigger. I have no worries that my wife and I will be able to give our two guests all they can eat and still leave plenty for all of us to back our carts up for a second serving.

I was once asked what was the difference between ordinary meat and game. Why did we hang game but not meat? The answer is perfectly simple. You do hang ordinary meat, or good butchers do. It would otherwise be tough and tasteless. You only hang meat for several days in a cool and airy place, though. You don't hang very young meat like veal for long or it goes slimy – or 'mosey' as we used to call it – and you don't hang very fat and flabby meat for the same reason.

44

Conventional game such as pheasants, partridges and hares are shot in winter, which is ideal for hanging them. They have been free to run the countryside long after they have passed the stage of being young and the exercise has prevented them from putting on any flabby fat. We hang our pheasants at least a fortnight and, when my wife has cooked them, they have the wonderful gamey flavour that only perfectly ripened and cooked meat possesses.

Good butchers hang beef or mutton for a week to ten days before cutting it up to put in the shop. Only those who patronise such old-fashioned craftsmen know what they are missing by buying modern mass-produced tack that is fit only for the stew pot, and only then after it has been camouflaged by 'Continental' cooking. The reason for such changes is that most meat is intensively reared and then killed and immediately hung on conveyor belts to be cut up and processed and packed in plastic bags almost before the victim 'has had time to breathe his last. It is then displayed on refrigerated slabs, cunningly lit to make it seem rosy and attractive, despite being as unripe as a half-grown crab apple.

Methods used in intensive farming and automated abattoirs have made proper butchering uneconomic and few of the modern generation ever learn to cook anything but 'convenience' foods. However, until we of the last generation tumble off our perches, there will still be a few around who know ways and means of ensuring that geese are not the foolish birds tradition would have us believe.

18. Rum Reminder of Those Good Old Days

Thumbing through an old diary, I was shattered to see that a radio programme called 'Country Christmas' was transmitted exactly thirty years ago. It didn't seem that long because every detail is etched in my mind so vividly that it could as easily have been last year. Our host was Bill Milner, a Shropshire farmer famous for the quality of his Hereford cattle. A party of countrymen met at his farm on Boxing Day morning, spent the day enjoying traditional country sports, met at the house for a party at night, and broadcast a programme about what we had done.

There was Frances Pitt, a famous naturalist who had written innumerable country books and contributed a column to a London evening paper for thirty-five years. Like so many naturalists of her generation, she was also a keen sports-woman and had been Master of the Wheatland Hounds for eight or ten years.

A venerable old fisherman went pike fishing, surely the most finger-numbing winter sport there is, and a naval officer, long past his pristine youth, went beagling. I suspected that this was to prove to himself that he was younger than his greying beard suggested and, judging by the heavy halo of naval rum fumes that surrounded him, I also reckoned that his presence in the hunting field would obliterate all scents of hare. The last members of the party were Percy Thrower and myself, who spent a pleasant day working off the effects of too much Christmas dinner by going ferreting for rabbits. How times have changed!

In those days, such country pursuits were taken for granted and the programme that ensued, describing our separate pleasures, never raised the faintest mutter of protest. If we did the same thing now, all hell would be let loose at half the party and half would go scot-free.

Miss Pitt, a most delightful and inoffensive countrywoman, would

Pike fishing, a finger-numbing winter sport which evokes no more passion than ratting in the breasts of 'antis', though the quarry's reactions must be the same as that of a salmon or a deer!

probably have found a demo at the meet. A few dozen bearded weirdos and flat-chested women in denims would have been bleating slogans about pastimes of the idle rich and a rent-a-mob of hunt saboteurs would have been dispensing modern anarchy by interfering with the lawful pursuits of others. The rummy breath of the naval officer out beagling would have been ignited by seafaring oaths, called down upon the heads of any who dared to try to divert him from his present course. But nobody would notice a couple of corduroy-trousered countrymen, with a bag of ferrets and disreputable terriers, or an ancient worthy with a fishing rod. Fishing and rabbiting are 'working men's' sports. Fox hunting and beagling are not!

I have every respect for the views of those who think 'blood' sports, as they call them, are cruel and should be stopped. The proper way to achieve their object is to persuade Parliament to pass laws to forbid them, not to take direct action which is likely to result in bloody noses and frayed tempers and only widens the sad rift that already splits town from countryside. And, if cruelty is the objection to hunting, there is no doubt that ratting and rabbiting and fishing and shooting are no better or worse than hunting. So why not ban them too?

The snag is that the question has become a political issue and, as there are said to be more fishermen than football fans, so many votes would be lost by opposing fishing that it would be professional suicide for MPs to tangle with chaps with fishing rods.

It is more emotive to paint hunting as the sport of the rich and privileged, and fishing and ratting as healthy pursuits of the masses and therefore inviolate.

Scientists at the germ warfare establishment at Porton Down have been commissioned by the Minister of Agriculture to devise a super poison for controlling foxes (and anything else that eats it!), which will exterminate them wholesale. I wonder if modern Reynards would look back on thirty years ago as the 'good old days', as I do?

19. On Kenched Backs

Boyhood friends in the Black Country would say that I'd 'got something come to my back'. Certainly every time I move it 'cops me i' the back'. I'm not sure if it is lumbago or if I have simply 'kenched' it.

A week ago, I was unloading hundredweight sacks of corn and tripped over a loose pebble on the floor while holding a sack in my arms. So, when I had difficulty in getting out of my chair by the fire to go to bed, I thought I'd kenched my back and that it would be easier by morning. That was over-optimistic. When the time came to get up, I had to roll out of bed on to the floor and scrabble up from there.

My wife, a sympathetic woman at heart, thought it was hilarious! Instead of getting better as the week wore on, it got worse, and all my friends joined in the fun and said that I *really* looked my age.

Tarka, my Rottweiler pup, always as sharp as a needle, immediately tumbled to the fact that I was now too slow to catch her a clip for not minding her manners, so she played me up for all she was worth. Normally steady to all livestock, she nipped into the paddock and caught a guinea pig, which was grazing there, and 'retrieved' it to hand as tenderly as a gun dog in a field trial. The guinea pig was not amused and emphasised the fact with loud and plaintive whistles, and the snag was that I was physically unable to bend down to accept Tarka's generous gift. It took some time to sort it out and I was astonished to see that the captive resumed his grazing the moment the pup condescended to set him free.

Tarka often finds a hen's egg and brings it to me as a present without so much as cracking the shell, and I was so pleased to confirm what a soft and tender mouth she has that I couldn't really be cross with her. I only wish she were as gentle when she is playing with me!

It wasn't until I could neither stand up nor bend down without provoking spasms of agony that I appreciated just how much we take such basic movements for granted.

49

I boil the dog meat every week in an old army cook pot over a Calor gas ring. The pot holds a couple of gallons of water and fifteen pounds or so of meat. I think nothing of it, normally – but my back did this time! I had to put water in the pot a pint or so at a time and drop the meat in hunk by hunk. Getting it out was far worse, producing such involuntary grunts and groans that I was sure it would delay recovery more than the week's interval that would signal the next cook-in.

The hens all laid eggs in the most inaccessible nests so that, when I bent down to pick them up, I thought I should never straighten my back again.

My father, who was an old-fashioned doctor, used to say that 'time was the most wonderful healer'. Embrocation and deep heat and massage, in his opinion, were left far behind by time to get things well. He was pretty crafty too, for he also knew that there is a certain cure for silly folk, like me, who do not give time a chance. 'You will, my lad,' he'd say, 'for pain's an equally good persuader.' He was dead right, of course.

I reckon to take the dogs round the wood two or three times a day, partly to exercise them and partly for my pleasure seeing the wildlife that shares it. Now my back aided the process. I am the world's best at never doing today what I can put off till tomorrow. The inevitable result is that pressure of work builds up and publishing deadlines creep up on me so that our leisurely strolls degenerate into mad gallops in order to get back to the typewriter that I sometimes feel rules my life. You can't gallop with a kenched back. You have to take things gently, however stridently duty calls, and the result has been that this last week our walks in the wood have been in slow motion and we have had time – and inclination! – to stand and stare much more than usual.

The mild winter has produced such an early season that we've admired snowdrops in bloom, honeysuckle in leaf, and birds singing as if spring had really sprung.

Now that my back has benefitted from time's healing, I'm going to adjust my priorities and take more time to appreciate the good things of life – without, I hope, any more pain to persuade me!

20. The Ruthless Bureaucrats*

Ministry of Agriculture scientists have now released details of the experiments they conducted to try to justify killing badgers that they allege transmit Bovine TB to cattle (*Veterinary Record*, December 11, 1982). Healthy badgers were caged in compounds and infected with TB. They were so frantic to escape that their yard had to be lined with concrete, six feet high, and the doors clad in steel.

Badgers are notoriously aggressive and fight bitterly for territory so that nothing could have been calculated to create worse stress. Even the scientists admitted that: 'TB is aggravated by stress, which may have shortened their lives.' Not only may it have shortened their lives but also increased their susceptibility to TB, making rubbish of the 'impartial' results. The festering wounds caused by fighting would have been the perfect medium for transmission.

Whether by ignorance or design, the experiments seem to have been loaded to make Brock the scapegoat. The standard of stockmanship was so disgraceful that one badger was not even missed until its carcase was found decomposing under a pile of hay, by which time the putrid tissue was 'unsuitable for examination'.

Even under such conditions, the calves penned with the badgers 'only acquired infection after at least six months' exposure to infected badgers'. The experimenters themselves say: 'In the field, the relative risk of cattle acquiring infection from badgers is low.' Nevertheless, the Ministry launched its attack on the evidence of those experiments.

In replies to recent questions in Parliament by Ivan Lawrence, MP for Burton, Peter Walker stated that the exercise costs the taxpayer £140,000 a year. A cool million since it began. A total of 4,478 setts have been gassed, which would kill a minimum of 15,000 badgers. This gassing was banned last year after intervention from a most unlikely source. Specialists at the Chemical Defence Establishment, at

51

* This article was originally published in February 1983.

Porton Down (famous for germ warfare) were briefed by Peter Walker to devise improvements in gassing techniques. Lord Zuckerman, who wrote a report on the subject, had wryly remarked that 'they' (Chemical Defence Establishment) 'are as well informed on the subject as any people in the country'.

Their first move was to establish just how effective the Ministry methods were – and they found the badgers took up to twenty-five minutes to die! They made no bones about the fact that the Ministry methods were unacceptably cruel and the Minister was forced to execute a humiliating U-turn and ban the gassing he had previously approved. This and the publication of the details of their laboratory techniques has effectively shattered Ministry credibility.

Bureaucracy is not easily deflected. When gassing was stopped, they switched to cage traps, which catch the animals alive, and so are said to be less brutal. The badgers might not have agreed because large numbers were sent to the Ministry concrete-lined compounds as subjects for experiment. Live trapping demands some skill, so the right was reserved to catch any badgers which proved 'trap-shy' in steel snares. Because badgers' heads are so small, these snares are often set to catch the animal round the belly where the wire soon digs in and causes dreadful lacerations. Hearing rumours that this type of capture was currently being practised in Staffordshire, I asked the Ministry spokesman for information. At first, he denied knowledge of the operation but subsequently phoned to say that trapping had never really stopped and that the policy is to keep freed areas clear.

I pointed out that badgers are now breeding and that captured sows would leave their orphaned cubs to starve. He said that this was 'emotive' but eventually promised that no sows would be removed from Staffordshire until the cubs were considered safely weaned. He could give no such assurance for the rest of the country.

The tragedy is that the callous campaign has no more chance of success than Canute had of stemming the tide. When badgers are cleared from an area, it is refilled from the surroundings, possibly by badgers from infected areas. A constructive alternative would be to produce a vaccine which could be fed in bait to make resident badgers safe and prevent colonisation by strange badgers from infected areas.

More advanced vets in Switzerland have already done this with foxes and rabies.

The impression gained from the Ministry campaign that badgers are vermin has encouraged an increase in illegal badger digging. Only last week several men in Cumbria were fined £700 apiece for digging out a badger, which one held by the tail while his son beat it over the head with the head of a spade until it died. It must be difficult to explain to the culprits why badger digging is so wicked while equally brutal actions by scientists are subsidised by taxpayers.

Concerned MPs, encouraged by the public, halted badger gassing. Similar Parliamentary pressure may yet stimulate constructive remedies instead of futile slaughter.

21. A Dog's Life

By February Tarka, my Rottweiler pup, was growing up. The police-dog trainer who introduced me to her breeder warned me that, though Rottweilers were among the most intelligent dogs that passed through his hands, they were also about the most headstrong. He said I would find her a challenge. How right he was! She is sweet-natured as a nun – but as rough and rumbustious as a Rugby League full-back!

For the first few weeks after she arrived, she played with me incessantly; her teeth were sharp as needles and she ripped my hands to ribbons. Dog breakers of the old school would have cured her instantly by thumping her hard enough to break her spirit. That was what they meant by dog *breaking*. I like my dogs to be close friends, not cringing slaves, and I was quite well aware that Rotts, as their friends call them, are very powerful and incredibly tough. Their ancestors had to be, for they were bred to herd cattle and were expected to put an obstreperous bull in his place when necessary. Their modern counterparts, used as police dogs, perform the same service for human villains.

You get what you pay for in this life, not only in cash but in kind. So I knew that my pup would have to go through the equivalent whizz-kid growing pains that human teenagers do before they settle down. My side of the bargain was that she, like all my dogs, has a life that must approach the canine ideal of perfection. Civilised behaviour will be the price she has to pay.

The greatest luxury a dog can have is almost constant human companionship. An ignorant criticism of those who train guide dogs for the blind is that it condemns the dogs to be perpetual servants. What rubbish! It gives them the closeness with their blind companion twenty-four hours a day. The most cruel thing one can do to a dog is to lock it up alone, either in a kennel or in an empty house. My dogs

54

Tarka and Belle in the sitting-room. Tarka loves her comforts

have a bonus. Not only do they spend the same long hours in my study as I do when I am working, but they come out in the wood with me when I take a break. And dogs love their walks as much as their comforts, companionship and good food!

I trained Tarka to be steady to stock while still such a puppy that I could run faster than she could if she chased a hen. But now that she is a husky nine-month-old bitch she is tasting the joys of the legitimate chase. It has been a terrible year for rats coming in out of the fields to the buildings around the house, so I have left a few long iron pipes around for them to dive into, to take cover if disturbed. Every evening I take the dogs out last thing before bedtime and they rush round the buildings to see if there are any rats about. Occasionally they find one in the open and catch him before he reaches safety but, more often, they run one into one of the pipes I have left around. All I have to do then is to shove a stick up the pipe and the dogs catch the rat when it bolts for what it hopes will be a safer place.

This puts ideas in the head of the young dog because it obviously arouses her hunting instinct, which lies not far below the surface of most dogs and many men! So I have to be very wary that a deer, suddenly erupting out of a thicket, does not put wrong ideas in her hitherto innocent canine mind. It keeps me on my mental toes because, so long as I am vigilant enough to spot forbidden quarry before the dog does, a sharp word of caution is all that is necessary. Prevention is easier than cure!

Comfort is, alas, very high on the priority list of all nice dogs, so young Tarka has discovered the charms of the most draught-proof easy chair. She sits in the sun, watching through the window the deer coming up to the birdtable, as if butter wouldn't melt in her mouth. In this respect it wouldn't, because she has now passed through her tiresome stage and she can be trusted not to blot her copybook, at least when I am there! She is discovering that, so long as she behaves, she has comfort and companionship, good food and sport. For her it really is a perfect dog's life.

22. A Boggy Battleground for Town and Country

The row about draining the Somerset Levels has emphasised the fact that relations between townsfolk and countrymen have never been at a lower ebb. The Somerset Levels comprise several thousand acres of some of the best grazing land in Britain. Huge acreages of water meadows, which are subject to flooding, are perfect for growing the roast beef of Old England but too soggy to plough for corn. The fact that they have never been ploughed means that a superb variety of wild flowers have colonised them naturally. A varied population of butterflies and other insects feed on the flowers, and birds and other wildlife feed on the insects.

The whole area is a veritable naturalists' paradise and thus proposals to drain it, so that it can be ploughed for corn, have started a conflict of extraordinary bitterness. Conservationists regard farmers there as money-grubbing vandals who wish to destroy their heritage to inflate their feather-bedded affluence. They point out that we are already growing so much more grain than we can sell economically that there is a mountain of the surplus. Because of the stupid Common Market habit of ignoring the laws of supply and demand, taxpayers have to pay for what the farmers do not sell.

The farmers regard their woolly-hatted critics as a bunch of interfering do-gooders. The land belongs to farmers and not to the knobbly-kneed butterfly hunters who seem to find it so easy to be generous with other people's way of life.

When the Nature Conservancy Council declared a large part of the area a Site of Special Scientific Interest the farmers were so furious that they hanged effigies of the conservationists and set fire to their shirt tails. In practice, a Site of Special Scientific Interest designation

The Somerset Levels in winter in full flood

carries little weight. All it does is to inform the owner that his land is important because it is the habitat of some important, or rare, plant or animal, and tells him what actions would be likely to damage it.

He is required, by law, to inform the Nature Conservancy Council before doing such potentially harmful operations so that efforts can be made to prevent what the conservationists regard as damage. In the last resort, a compulsory purchase order might be slapped on his land.

I can see both sides of the argument, which is not always helped by the Nature Conservancy Council itself. Like most bureaucrats, they tend to throw their arrogant weight about, and I mistook one youth, sent to 'survey' my own wood, for a youth experience trainee, though he may have been adequate as an armchair boffin in a laboratory, with text books at his elbow. If there were many like him on the Somerset Levels, I am not surprised at the farmers' actions!

But the quarrels seem to me to go far deeper than opposition to draining a few thousand acres of boggy meadows. The countryside has been changing continuously for thousands of years. In prehistoric times, most of the lowlands were covered in woods which were gradually cleared and burned to give way to agriculture. Most of the field hedgerows were only planted during the enclosures a couple of centuries ago, to give the lovely patchwork of fields that are so beloved by conservationists.

It is the earthmoving equipment, developed during the last war, that has really revolutionised the landscape. Huge bulldozers have carved motorways across the face of the land, electric pylons and cables have stitched their way from power station to power station, and draglines and diggers have made it simple to deepen rivers and drain bogs.

Changes that have been happening over centuries have suddenly accelerated out of control, destroying the habitat for wildlife and making it possible to grow crops for which there is no market. Farmers want to cash in; conservationists yearn to stem the tide and turn the land into a museum, freezing it as inanimate as trout in aspic.

We are in an industrial revolution far more severe than the advent of steam engines two centuries ago. If we do not master machines, machines will master us.

23. *Countrymen of the Future*

About April every year, I get a trickle of letters from youngsters anxious about their future. As the summer term wears on and the end of the school year approaches, the trickle swells into a torrent. Because I earn my living in the countryside, readers of my books and viewers of my television programmes believe that I can get them fixed up with a satisfying job, far away from the bustling rat race they often see around them.

Some want to be gamekeepers or stockmen. Others hanker after a life working with trees, far from crowds and human pressures. A nice job as the warden of a nature reserve sounds very appealing, and glamorous pictures of girls with cuddly lambs in their arms that always appear at daffodil time inevitably produce a crop of would-be shepherdesses. The nostalgia for rural life and simple things is a reaction to our mass-producing throwaway society – but I am sad to say that it is beyond my power to help because such attractive, worthwhile ways of earning a living are harder and harder to get.

The boffins are always inventing clever ways of taking the irk out of work. What once took hundreds of hours with a pick and shovel now takes as many minutes with a mechanical digger. Tractors and multi-furrow ploughs do more in a day than a ploughman plodding his weary furrow behind a team of horses could do in a week. The modern ploughman sits in comfort in his heated tractor cab, with earphones on to damp out the mechanical noise and provide the dulcet Irish brogue of Gloria Hunniford instead. Gone are the aching muscles and rain-sodden clothes. Gone the chores of rubbing down sweaty horses and mucking out smelly stables.

Although tractor ploughing takes considerable skill, there is not quite the same satisfaction in ploughing a straight furrow that seems to disappear into infinity now, as there was doing so behind straining

60

horses, when it demanded almost the same concentration to walk upright along a squelching furrow as it did to steer an undeviating course to the horizon.

It is the same with so many of the other jobs that youngsters want. Nearly all stock is now farmed intensively, with mechanical scrapers to clean the floors of sheds or slurry pits and to catch the waste that is then pumped into tanks and spewed on to the land by one man, doing the work of ten of his ancestors. Chain saws and cranes have transformed skilled foresters into equally skilled mechanics who are now the servants instead of the masters of machines.

We all blame unemployment on the recession or militant unions or bad management. The real villain of the piece is the machine, for we are in the midst of an industrial revolution as basic as the last one, when steam engines made craftsmanship give way to mass production by mechanical marvels in factories. This time it has spread to the countryside. Juggernaut earth-moving machinery has sounded the death knell of navvies with picks and shovels. The back-breaking task of lifting sugar beet by hand, or clearing waterlogged ditches with muscle-tearing toil was hell, at the time, and I have no doubt that modern draining machines would have been as welcome as vacuum cleaners after the dustpan and brush.

But craftsmen who are demoted to mere machine minders cannot be blamed for putting on their rose-tinted specs to look back to the past with nostalgia. Sooner or later, we shall have to face the fact that we will have to decide whether machines are to be our masters or our slaves. If one machine is to do what ten men did, then nine of those ten will have to be kept by the tenth. If we are sensible, and make machines our slaves, we may all be able to lead more civilised lives with far more leisure, provided that we are content to be competitive by taking no more out of the kitty than our competitors. In that case, the next generation may be able to settle for doing less dull, mechanical, repetitive work than we do and have more leisure for the simple things in country life that my postbag tells me so many of them crave.

24. *Lambing in Cold Comfort?*

No sight delights my eyes more than a field of playful lambs in spring. At first glance they look all legs, as if they would be somewhat ungainly, but they can skim over the grass in an easy galloping stride. They love to find a fallen tree trunk or mound of soil on which to play king-of-the-castle. First one will jump up and lower his head, as fierce as a bull in a Spanish bull ring, threatening his fellows with an almighty battering if they so much as dare to challenge his supremacy. But the threat is empty and he flees for his life as soon as one of his fellows rushes up to challenge him. As he descends, his fellows chase him and the procession circles the tree trunk with all the abandon of human kids escaping from school.

To get the full enjoyment of such capers, the sun should be shining and primroses and wild violets and daffodils should be in bloom. Lambs just don't look right in unseasonable weather.

This spring has been a real shocker. The weathermen have had an easy time because all they have had to predict has been rain, followed by more rain, to be bang on target. Our land is cold and clammy clay at the best of times and I have never seen it soggier. It has been the wettest April that I can remember.

A visitor from London walked around the wood with me last week and exclaimed with delight that she hadn't had such a good 'squelch' since she was a kid on holiday at an uncle's farm. The local lambs would not have agreed. When we came, twenty or so years ago, there were mighty few lambs in the district. The land in our part of the country is famous for dairy cows but used to be considered too cold and wet for sheep.

One of the idiotic aspects of the Common Market is that farmers are persuaded to grow mountains of surplus food and produce lakes of surplus milk under commercially unsuitable conditions. Taxpayers

An unusually large family – these four were born to a grey-face Dartmoor ewe on a farm near Newton Abbot in Devon

featherbed them with subsidies to grow crops that nobody wants, where such crops would not be grown if they had to stand or fall by simple profit and loss. This has caused vast capital sums to be laid out to keep pigs and poultry under factory-farming conditions that give them neither a dignified nor a comfortable life.

Sheep are slightly different. When I was growing up, sheep were running out all winter, as they still do in the hill country of Wales and Scotland and the Lake District. Although their fleece is liberally larded with natural lanolin, making them almost completely weather-proof, they suffer great hardship in deep and prolonged snow. If the weather is foul when they lamb, the lambs die off in dozens. Although each ewe may have two lambs, anything above an average of one lamb reared is counted acceptable.

There is more shelter in our part of the country but the soil is so heavy and impervious that it holds the wet and would soon be trodden into a quagmire by the sharp cloven hooves of sheep. So farmers have used some of the Common Market subsidy to make large, covered buildings, with concrete floors, where sheep can be yarded in comfort all winter and only turned out, with their young lambs, when spring sunshine beckons. It is one of the few intensive farming practices that makes life more tolerable for livestock as well as more profitable for the farmers.

The best-laid schemes do not always conform to plan! Mating time is calculated to produce the crop of lambs just as the young grass would be shooting and the sun would be shining. The sheep yard is just big enough to house the ewes, but they had to be turned out when the lambs were three days old. The sun didn't shine and it bucketed down with drenching rain, chilling the lambs through their theoretically waterproof fleeces. Instead of romping with the joys of spring, they wandered forlornly round their pasture, vainly seeking shelter.

Only the strongest have survived to enjoy a belated sunny spell. Sheep yards and Common Market subsidies are no match for Nature.

25. *Pigeon Flyers Put Ministry in a Spin**

The men from the Ministry are crying 'wolf' again. This time their quarry are the pigeon-flyers, who begin racing their birds from the Continent in May. The excuse for banning the sport is that there have been reports of Newcastle disease among pigeons on the Continent, which might be spread here if our birds are sent over to be liberated at the start of a race.

Newcastle disease – or Paramyxovirus-3, if you prefer to be blinded with science – is better known as the fowl pest that caused thousands of poultry to be slaughtered here. So, on the face of it, it seems sensible to take every precaution to prevent an epidemic. Closer examination, though, reveals that reports of the disease in Belgium and Germany turned out to be a misdiagnosis of paratyphoid.

The policy of our Ministry of Agriculture when such diseases occur is not vaccination, but mass slaughter. However, the Ministry destroyed its credibility when Agriculture Minister Peter Walker had to ban badger gassing which his own men had practised for seven years – because the germ warfare department at Porton Down (of all people!) said it was unacceptably cruel.

So the pigeon-racers are naturally sceptical about the competence of the boffins at the Ministry who want to stop their sport. They say the Ministry is forbidding it because the French will not give an assurance that there is no Newcastle disease in France. It so happens that the French are unhappy that we will not allow them to send cheap poultry into the country to undercut our prices. Perhaps it is cynical to wonder if the French are not getting a bit of their own back?

When there was last an outbreak of Newcastle disease among poultry, the policy here was slaughter, with compensation, rather than vaccination as on the Continent. Some poultry farmers, with flocks

* This article was originally published in May 1983.

A racing pigeon hitches a lift on the Dieppe/Newhaven ferry!

that had just about come to the end of their useful, productive lives, were laughing all the way to the bank.

The Ministry's methods of dealing with the 1967 foot-and-mouth epidemic were equally suspect. Carcasses of cattle killed to prevent the spread of the disease were burned on huge fires. But some scientists claimed that warm air rising when the fire was first lit carried the virus into the clouds – to be spread elsewhere – before the heat was intense enough to destroy all life.

So how sensible are the Ministry's suggestions now? It appears to have no answer to the fact that, if domestic racing pigeons could bring the plague from the Continent, so could migrating wild birds. There is a constant shuttle of wood pigeons and starlings from overseas, to say nothing of the seasonal migratory birds. Nor does the Ministry provide any proof that Newcastle disease has ever been spread to poultry by pigeons, which has always been the reason given on previous occasions. This time, it says, it is being cruel to be kind to the pigeons of the country – though it can do nothing to control far greater numbers of wild birds.

There are a lot of pigeon-flyers, each with a vote, so the bureaucrats don't want to offend them too much. So they say that birds can be put on a ship, taken out into the Bay of Biscay and liberated from there. They have no answer to the fact that there would be nothing to prevent them making landfall in France on the way home. To make the best of a bad job, the pigeon men are sending birds by fleets of transporters to Land's End.

So, if you are going on holiday down south and get on the end of a queue of transporters down Devonshire lanes, think of the Men from the Ministry, to pass away the time!

26. *Tarka – From Pup to Guard Dog*

One of the risks in having a new dog is that it won't hit it off with the old one. Although I feel half-dressed without a dog, and in more than sixty years have never been without one, a roll-call of their names would be less than a baker's dozen. Once they have been accepted as members of our household, they have been part of the family for life. With the exception of Grip and Rebel, two Staffordshire bull terriers, whose ancestors had been bred for fighting, they all settled down pretty well.

Grip and Rebel, the best ratting dogs I ever saw, blew their tops because they both tried to get through a half-open door at the same time when they heard me return from work. Each thought the other was trying to reach me first and, although they were dog and bitch, they set on to fight as viciously as human prizefighters. I choked them apart before too much damage was done, but they were never again safe to leave together without supervision. When they died, I replaced them with gentler breeds.

Tick, the German short-haired pointer who shared my life for twelve years, was such a favourite that another of the same breed, bringing back too vivid memories, would not have stood a chance. So Tarka, the Rottweiler, joined the family a year ago. She was just over seven weeks old, too tiny even to climb into the dog box by the radiator in the kitchen. The police-dog trainer, who found her for me, warned that the breed are very wilful and that I would find my new pup a challenge to train. It was an understatement.

She is immensely intelligent and delightfully affectionate ... but although it is simple to make her understand what is wanted, that is only half the battle. If I was bright enough to make Tick understand what I wanted, it was her pleasure to comply, but the same willingness is shown by Tarka only if it is what she wants too. It would, of course, have been simple enough to have knocked compliance into her or snatched it in with one of the modern choke-chains, which look less brutal than old-fashioned dog whips because they don't leave a mark, but that is not my way. I want my dogs faithful as friends, not zombies, and I find that limitless patience always does the trick in the end, and my new pup is showing every sign of being as good as my last.

There has been one serious worry. Belle, the Alsatian, is a gentle-natured, affectionate bitch but not a strong personality – except when strangers trespass. Then she stands no nonsense whatsoever. But Tick always dominated her and, although they were very good friends, there was never any doubt about which of them was top dog. Belle treated Tarka, when she arrived, like a delicate doll, to be fondled and played with. The pup could do no wrong, whether it was hanging

Tarka and Belle are steady to domestic stock and wildlife. Their only permitted quarry are rats, rabbits and squirrels. Here they have treed a squirrel

onto her long tail, pulling her ears or nicking goodies from her dinner.

Soon the pup grew into a hefty lump of muscle, with teeth still as sharp as needles. I left the old bitch to establish the peck order and would not have remonstrated if she had put the upstart well and truly in her place, but she took everything that was coming to her without complaint. So I ticked the pup off and stopped her, but she bounced back like India rubber and the old bitch was as offended as if it was her that I had scolded. It got to the stage where the pup dominated the old lady until she was utterly demoralised, refusing to come for walks and going off her food.

Now, I am delighted to say, it is all ending happily. The turning point came when the pup got her second teeth (which are not so needle-sharp) and lost her playfulness as she matured. They have suddenly found that they have more serious interests in common, and love ratting in the yard at night, or coming for walks in the wood. They even share delicacies from the same plate.

Although Rottweilers are used as police dogs in Germany, Tarka is so good natured that she welcomed strangers at first – but that is changing too. When they are the other side of the fence, she bares her teeth, roars her defiance, and Belle joins in the chorus. It is the start of another delightful partnership.

27. *Rough Justice!*

We've had problems with our first row of peas. As soon as the grains had sprouted, they appeared on the surface, well and truly chewed up. It wasn't the birds, because the whole row had been carefully covered with a pea-guard of fine wire-netting to protect them, but even fine wire-netting is no safeguard against mice. They simply burrow under the edge. So I set a 'nipper' mousetrap each end, under the guard, and landed a fine brace of long-tailed fieldmice next morning. I repeated the tactic, day after day, and caught a grand total of twenty-one reinforcements as soon as they were mustered for the attack.

That first row of peas is rather more blanks than prizes, the second row is coming through and I collected a couple of casualties before breakfast this morning. You might think, therefore, that I would be delighted to see a potential ally, in the form of a stoat, running across the lawn that borders the kitchen garden.

All the books say that fieldmice are among the favourite prey of stoats so, since stoats have more time and incentive to go hunting than I do, they ought to be able to control our plague of rodents more effectively than I can. The snag is that stoats will scoff almost anything that they can catch – and at this time of year there are easier things to catch than agile mice. Young birds, for example.

The next time I saw the stoat, it was crossing the lawn again, bearing in triumph the corpse of a bedraggled young thrush. The third time we met was unlucky for the stoat. In the wood, a couple of hundred yards from the house, there is a pile of logs, under a corrugated iron shelter, where we stack them to season for winter fuel. As I went past, with the dogs, they stopped and tested the breeze with sensitive noses before making a bee-line for the log pile.

Belle, the Alsatian, is a powerful bitch and large logs scattered in

A stoat and his prey, a rabbit over twice his size

all directions. From the depth of the pile a high-pitched chatter screamed abuse at her and the air grew thick with the musky pong that stoats give off to drive enemies away. This scent, stored in glands under stoats' tails, is the same scent that women use to turn men on – though considerably diluted – but the concentrated stench around our woodpile certainly did nothing for me. Even the stoat hadn't got ultimate faith in its effectiveness because his confidence sagged and he left the comparative safety of his sanctuary and made a bolt for it. Belle was too quick for him and now the rest of the brood of thrushes stand a better chance of survival. So, for that matter, do my chickens that are growing up in the paddock.

All the same, I am illogically fond of stoats and weasels. They are so lithe and graceful that it would be churlish not to admire them, and I suppose that the surplus of young birds and mice and voles are their crop, to be harvested, as much as peas are a crop, to be harvested by mice and men – whoever gets there first!

There is nothing sentimental about Nature and most creatures survive simply by breeding a surplus so that a few of the fittest can win against long odds.

28. Stop Beefing about the Bull*

I have always regarded ramblers as reasonable people who have every respect for the law, so that it came as a surprise to hear an official spokesman for the Ramblers Association inciting his members to trespass on private property. The cause was the hoary question of loose bulls in fields crossed by public footpaths.

The recent 1983 Wildlife and Countryside Act states that bulls of breeds predominantly bred for milk production shall not be left loose in fields to which the public has access. But bulls of 'beef' breeds may be allowed to run freely with their cows, even if there is a footpath. That is what the ramblers are beefing about.

Like so many conflicts between townsfolk and countrymen, the differences of opinion are based on ignorance and it is a sad fact that, as we get more and more leisure and easier transport, the gulf between town and country shows every sign of growing wider and deeper.

Examine, for a moment, the reasoning behind the clause about loose bulls in the Wildlife and Countryside Act. The fact that some breeds of cattle are famous for beef while others produce more milk is no accident. Each breed has been evolved by generations of careful selective breeding for a specific purpose. It is a great achievement that the best milking cows can give ten to twelve gallons a day. When I was a lad, it was a good cow that could give six. Selective breeding, to give such improvement, is always a matter of compromise. Some qualities have to be sacrificed in order to achieve the others. In the case of top-class milking cows, the quality of beef is not so good as in beef breeds – and the temper of the bulls is often notorious. This is not particularly important with milking cows because they have to come to be milked every day, so that the cowman knows precisely when they are in season and ready for mating. The bull can be kept in a pen, where he can do no damage, and the cowman can introduce

* This article was originally published in July 1983.

the cows to him on exactly the day when conception is most likely.

Cattle that have been bred for generations to provide beef are traditionally poor milkers, but it so happens that their bulls are sweet-tempered and docile. Breeding cattle of beef breeds do not need the concentrated special feeding of milk cattle, so that they spend most of their lives grazing in fields, where the cowman cannot tell when they are ripe for mating. Only the bull can do that in the open and, by happy coincidence, loss of sweet temper was not one of the factors that had to be sacrificed to produce the best beef. So the farmer can get his beef cows in calf simply by running their bull with them, and leaving the rest to Nature.

The open country best suited for beef production is frequently both beautiful and criss-crossed by footpaths, which were often made originally to let friends and neighbours take short cuts to school or market, not as leisure trails for strangers. If bulls were precluded from sharing the pastures with cows, it might be quite impossible to get the cows in calf.

The clause in the Wildlife and Countryside Act allowing loose bulls of gentle breeds in such circumstances seems perfectly reasonable, and few who understood the countryside would wish to jeopardise the livelihood of beef breeders rather than pass through a field containing a harmless bull.

The same man who was bellyaching about loose bulls complained equally about farmers who grow corn crops across footpaths. The countryside is, and always has been, a patchwork of changing patterns. Existing paths often went along hedgerows, but the original hedges have since been removed to cater for modern machinery. Surely it would be sensible to move with the times by diverting paths to fit modern farming practice?

Militant extremists who incite others to flout the law simply destroy their own cause in the eyes of responsible people.

29. *Wise Dogs and Idiot Owners*

Having enjoyed twelve years of unswerving loyalty and affection from my old German pointer Tick, I simply could not imagine anyone who could be cruel to such a dog. So a letter from a reader really set my teeth on edge. Like me, she is an enthusiast for the breed and has discovered that some of them are so badly treated that it has been necessary to set up the German Short-haired Pointer Rescue Service. It is a voluntary organisation whose objects are to find suitable homes for German pointers who are not being properly looked after. In its first year, it has rescued between fifty and sixty dogs. Five were beyond help, including two convicted sheep worriers, for once a dog has acquired a taste for sheep on the hoof, it can never be trusted again.

In passing, I would say that I would not trust *any* dog not to chase and worry sheep, if left unsupervised or, worse still, allowed to wander the countryside in company with another dog. Sheep are natural prey for dogs. They positively incite attack by rushing away in panic.

One of the 'failures' had been confined to a tiny balcony on the eighth floor of a block of flats and two more had endured such terrible conditions that they, too, had gone mad and, like the sheep worriers, had to be destroyed. The rest, though, have been found kind homes, where they are now not only happy themselves, but giving happiness to their new owners. Homes have to be found for a few dogs whose owners die or are ill or move where dogs are not allowed, but the genuine 'rescues' are usually due more to lack of imagination than sheer cruelty.

A few addle-headed oafs buy dogs for Christmas or birthdays without a thought for what they will do with them when holidays come round. Being banished to the strange surroundings of boarding kennels is traumatic enough for any sensitive dog, but some louts, who should never be allowed to keep a dog at all, simply turn them loose,

If ignorant owners could see the results, they might think twice before letting their dogs loose on farmland. Otherwise, they should not be surprised if their pooches are shot

often miles from home, to save the cost of boarding. Such people must have such low mentality that I often wonder what could possibly have sired an idea as original as having a dog, and how they decided what breed to choose.

Letters I get during the run of a television series like *One Man and His Dog* often worry me very much. People who see the wonderful intelligence of collies shepherding sheep are suddenly urged to have a collie of their own, however unsuitable the place in which they live. They do not seem to realise that highly-intelligent dogs need owners with the skill and specialist knowledge to be accepted as 'pack leader' or the dog will take command himself. Dogs capable of running up hill and down dale, shepherding sheep all day, need far more exercise than the average owner can give them, so I do my best to put such prospective owners off. Nevertheless, the soaring price of collies is some indication that demand has far outstripped supply.

Not only farmers but also the National Trust and other landowners have
problems with sheep worrying

Another clue is the fact that a rescue service for Old English Sheep-
dogs (the ones that appear in paint ads) had to deal with 3,000 cases
last year. My old Tick was on the box twenty-five or thirty times and
I hate to think that her obvious attractions seduced unsuitable folk to
try to buy one like her.

Now I do all in my power to ensure that people who choose dogs
see not only the joys they bring but also the responsibilities.

30. Murine Tycoon?

I started wheeler-dealing early in life. Pence, as pocket money, were few and far apart so what money I had, I had to make for myself. A pair of white mice set me up in business on my seventh birthday. An evilly-disposed older cousin presented them to me with the impish intention of seeing how I coped with parental opposition when my room began to reek of mice. He was disappointed because I was sharp enough to keep them well out of sight, in the potting shed at the bottom of the garden, so the family never suspected that I had acquired such smelly pets. I had great fun looking after them all the holidays – but the crunch came when I had to go back to school next term.

We weren't allowed pets at my prep school and I had no illusions about the chances of success if I asked my father or mother to look after them while I was away! So I made a rather complicated 'house' for them in a long wooden box, which I stuffed with cotton wool I scrounged from the Old Man's surgery. It was a luxury home for mice, by any standards, and I hid it in a corner of the fowl pen, where they could lie in five-star, feather-bedded luxury all day and come out to feed on corn, left by the poultry, at night. It worked like a dream.

My first call, when I came home for the holidays, was to the fowl pen, to see if my beloved mice had survived. Not only had they survived, they had multiplied. My long wooden box was now divided into a number of nests, and squirming mice, of all sizes and colours, scattered in all directions. I left them alone to creep back to the 'safety' of their box, quietly stopped up the entrance, and winkled them out, one at a time, into a cardboard box. I took this down to the local pet shop and flogged them to the unsuspecting owner, who naturally imagined they were tame, whereas all but the original pair had been brought up like ordinary wild mice. The cash I collected was the first capital of a budding entrepreneur, so I spent part of my holiday making an improved-model breeding quarters for next term's stock! The capital I had amassed, from the progeny of the original mice, was invested in more and higher-class stock to produce more and better mice to sell next holidays.

My production costs were at rock bottom, because the food was free, scrumped from the surplus that the poultry was rash enough to leave ungleaned overnight. But, like most get-rich-quick schemes, I soon hit a snag that taught me there is no such place as Easy Street. The production side of the business was efficiency itself, but I found myself enmeshed in marketing difficulties! Pet-shop owners who are besieged by angry mums, bewailing the fact that their cosseted brats have been bitten by what were sold to them as tame mice, have to refund the purchase price. I found, when I returned with fresh stock next holidays, that there was no 'Welcome' on the pet-shop mat, and finding new outlets would soon have put me out of business.

So, like other wheeler-dealers, I cut my losses and switched to larger animals, with fatter profit margins, like ferrets, which I persuaded a gardener at school to keep during term, in exchange for being allowed to use them for rabbiting on Sundays.

I am often reminded of my early forays into commerce by a freak strain of wild, long-tailed fieldmice that inhabit my land. Like most stock-keepers, I'm pretty hard on mice and rats which raid my corn, and about eight years ago I was astonished to find an odd-coloured fieldmouse in one of my traps. It wasn't quite white, but its coat was a beautiful pale cream. The fact that its eyes were pink indicated that it was almost, if not quite, albino. I didn't think much about it at the time, assuming that it was a one-in-a-thousand exception that would prove the rule that Nature's laws of heredity would make such characters recessive so that they would soon die out. But our white wild mice never have died out and I have grown so attached to them that I only cage-trap in the corn store – and let my white ones go again!

Perhaps I am a sentimental old fool, harking back to fantasies of childhood. Or perhaps it is a shrewd business to build up a stock of rarities that, one day, may be worth their weight in gold to the fanciers of white mice!

31. Modern Featherbed Farmers*

Common Market farmers are producing far more than their customers are prepared to buy. There is enough wine to give all Europe a hangover and enough milk to drown an army in the surplus milk lake or to engulf it in a butter bog. The reason for such nonsense is that we have allowed the financial gnomes to get the whip hand and manipulate prices without regard to the basic laws of supply and demand. They have created such lunacy that more than two-thirds of the Community's annual budget is being squandered to produce embarrassing surpluses. Some £10,000 million out of a total budget of £15,000 million is poured into agricultural pouches.

Between now and Christmas, the Finance and Agricultural Ministers of the Community will be wrangling among themselves to try to restore sanity at each other's expense. But the farming lobby is ruthless and powerful, as politicians have discovered to their cost.

Stanley Evans, MP for Wednesbury, made his number after the last war and was appointed junior minister at the Ministry of Food. Food, in those days, was dear for much the same reasons as it is today except that, instead of having grain mountains and milk lakes to bolster prices artificially, there were genuine shortages as the aftermath of war. Evans made a memorable speech, castigating farmers, who he described as being 'feather-bedded'. Poor chap. He never knew what hit him. Before he knew where he was, he was out on his ear, after a ministerial career of only sixty days.

We could do with a few more like him today. There are so many small French farmers that the number of their votes could rock the Gallic boat, so old Mitterrand panders to them as shamelessly as did Giscard before him. Margaret Thatcher does not suffer such foolishness gladly but her Ministers of Agriculture have been poor tools, by comparison, so may not have had their hearts as much in the fight as she would.

80

* This article was originally published in October 1983.

Farming is Big Business: harvest scene near Braintree in Essex. (The 1984 EEC grain mountain stood at approximately 20 million tons)

Before getting tough with the foreigners, it is really vital to put their own house in order – and there never was a better time. British farmers have blotted their copybooks in so many ways that the public is in no mood to be rooked as well. The sad thing is that small farmers, on marginal land, really do need higher prices, in one form or another, to make a living, and some form of subsidy for farming marginal land is one way of achieving it.

Private landowners have been deterred from letting their land to tenant farmers because once a farm has been let to a tenant it is virtually impossible to repossess it – even if the owner needs it for himself or for his family. When a large landowner dies and his family have to pay death duties, it often becomes necessary to sell off part of his estate – which is worth far less tenanted than it would have been with vacant possession. The obvious result has been that, when farm tenants have died and the tenancy has fallen in, the tendency has been for owners to take the land over and farm it themselves.

But some of the largest and most profitable farms are not farmed by conventional farmers at all. They are owned by big corporations and pension funds and trades unions, who simply regard them as items on their balance sheet, and employ highly efficient managers to farm them as profitably as possible, regardless of ethics. Some of the worst cases of soulless factory farming are found on huge farms that the owners never see, except as figures in a book.

If seven battery hens can produce more eggs than six, the owners never see the misery they create. Cows, milked three times a day and discarded as so much scrap machinery when they wear themselves out with lactating, are a profitable enterprise, so long as taxpayers subsidise the milk they could not sell on the open market. Fertile water meadows, which have reared countless generations of superb beef cattle, are drained to grow corn that is in surplus before the expensive operation even begins.

It isn't expensive to the farmer, of course, because taxpayers pay for it – and conservationists cry vainly over the loss of wildlife that relies for existence on wetlands that are growing annually scarcer. So much corn is now grown that straw, once vital as a fertiliser, is sent up in flames which shower smuts more deadly than tobacco smoke.

Farming has become Big Business instead of a respected way of life. So farmers mustn't grumble if taxpayers insist that it is treated on a business footing and the laws of supply and demand are allowed to replace subsidies that have feather-bedded them too long.

32. *Bolts from the Blue*

A thunderbolt hit the junction box in the drive where our phone wire comes across to the house and knocked the phone out for five days last week. It was quite impressive at the time, because a very loud crack literally coincided with a brilliant orange flash that floodlit the kitchen as bright as a pantomine set. The guts of the junction box were fused to metallic icicles and the insulation on the wires melted like butter in the sun.

I often think the telephone is one of the curses of our civilisation because strangers persist in intruding on my privacy just when I'm trying to concentrate. If the whole system seized up, it would surely be a blessing! The gilt soon wore off when it did! I didn't mind nobody being able to bother me but the fact that I was not able to bother anyone else was quite a different matter.

I suppose it wouldn't have been so inconvenient in a town because towns seem littered with phone boxes. But there's only one in our village, which is a mile away from the house. Whenever I went there was always some wench, curled up in comfort, conducting interminable conversations that must have been hilariously funny, to judge by her belly-shaking brays of mirth that almost made the phone box rock in rhythm.

Everybody knows everything in a village, so the postmistress, who lives opposite, came out to see why I was loitering outside the phone box. 'You should pay your bill, then,' was all the sympathy I got.

When the wench in the box eventually ran out of two-bob pieces and had to emerge to replenish her supply, I was just feeling ripe to deal with British Telecom. My phone had already been reported out of order, I was told. They obviously couldn't care less, but they wouldn't last five minutes if there was any competition.

My neighbour, on the farm next door, was in the same plight, only

83

he was awakened at half-past two in the morning by a mechanical apparition, roaring up like a helicopter with brightly flashing lights. It turned out to be an agricultural contractor who had turned up with a special combine harvester to reap the oil-seed rape. Such contractors work twenty-four hours a day, in the rush of harvest time, and he apologised for not warning of his middle-of-the-night arrival, but he couldn't get through on the phone. Did my neighbour know it was out of order? He certainly did, and he wished that British Telecom would get stuck in and work twenty-four hours a day as well, and get a bit of service on the go.

When it comes to hard practice, idyllic rural life is not always as enchanting as it is painted in theory. The thunderstorm that knocked out the phone for five long days knocked off the electricity for as many hours. No great hardship in summer, you might think, but the uncertainties of the duration raise doubts about the grub in the deep freeze, that has taken so much time and effort to grow, and decent programmes on the television always coincide with power cuts.

But, despite the discomforts of the storms, I was relieved to see the rain. We get our water on a shared pipeline across almost a mile of fields. It wasn't too bad when we came, twenty years ago, as the two farms who shared the supply only milked a few cows. But both have herds of about one hundred now, and one milks his three times a day – so there aren't many hours when one or other is not either milking, washing down the sheds or encouraging the cows he has just milked to top themselves up with liquid for the next milking time.

The result is that demand has so far outstripped supply that, for several hours a day, nothing comes out of our tap. I wrote to the chief engineer of the water authority a week ago, asking politely for our inadequate supply to be improved, but so far have not received the courtesy of a reply. Perhaps he was trying to phone me when the phone didn't work.

33. Sordid Trade

A skulk of disreputable characters sneaked past our house most autumn Sunday mornings sixty years ago. I was an innocent-looking little lad at the time but often followed them, to see what they were at. I disguised my intentions by pretending to be chasing butterflies but, in any case, I was too young to pose any threat and they took no notice of me. Some of them played cards or dice among the worked-out pit mounds on Bentley Common, a mile or so away, for gambling in public was illegal in those days. Sometimes they would take game cocks from bags hidden under their jackets and retreat to hollows among the gorse bushes, in which case they always left a lookout, high on a mound, where he could see if there were any coppers stalking them.

They had a curiously courteous attitude to me because I was 'the doctor's son'. They thought they mustn't swear in front of me but, on the other hand, it would have been unthinkable to have referred to a policeman without showing antagonism. So, they never asked me if I'd seen the bloody copper, which would have been disrespectful, they compromised by inquiring if I'd seen any 'red' coppers around.

The thistles were seeding at this time of year, and goldfinches, the 'seven-coloured linnets' that bird fanciers so loved, gathered in flocks or 'charms' to feed on the seeds before they floated away on thistle-down. Some of the chaps who congregated among the spoil heaps had nets, worked at a distance by pulling cords, and in each net was a bird in a cage. When others came down, to see why one of their fellows was piping his heart out in a tiny prison, the net was sprung and they, too, were captives for the rest of their lives. Others were caught by the even more barbarous practice of spreading a sticky substance, called bird-lime, on the twigs.

If you think such conduct was confined to the bad old days, you

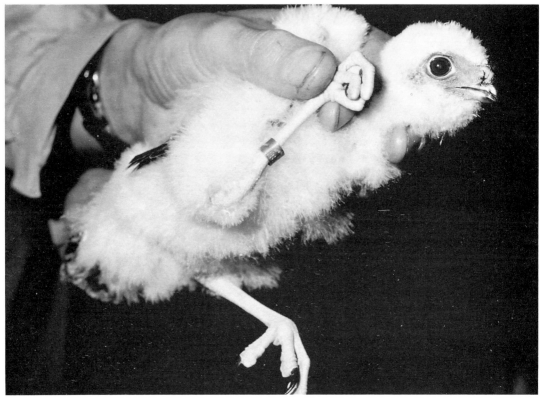

A young sparrow hawk, ringed before it is too large for the ring to slip over its foot to 'prove' that it was bred in captivity. Some dealers ring wild hawks still in the nest, then return to take them illegally before they fledge

are wrong. You could buy a seven-coloured linnet for a few pence in the 1920s. The false values of our affluent society now put a thousand pounds on the head of a peregrine falcon but such noble hawks are still for sale on the squalid black market. There are plenty of louts around who will sell their souls for less than that.

The Wildlife and Countryside Act was conceived in the pious hope that, among other noble causes, capturing wild hawks would be made illegal by law with enough teeth to be effective. Unfortunately the boffins who drafted the law were so ignorant that the clause they relied on does nothing. They believed that, if they made it illegal to

A male goshawk on the arm of a falconer. Note the jesses attached to his legs

buy or sell, or have in your possession, a hawk that was not 'close-rung' and registered, they would restrict the possession of hawks and other wild birds to those which had been bred in captivity. This is because close-ringing means putting a solid ring, with no gap, on to the leg of the bird. This can only be done when the bird is so young and small that the ring will slip over its foot. By the time it is a few days old, the foot will be too large to go through the ring so that, in theory, ringing will be proof that the bird was bred in captivity.

If the boffins had seen the bird catchers of my youth, they would have realised what rubbish this is. Old timers would find a lark's nest, wait until the young were almost ready to fly, and then put an ordinary garden riddle over the nest. The young birds couldn't get out but their parents could see and feed them through the wire mesh of the riddle. The bird catchers let the old birds go on feeding them till they were self-supporting, when they took them home, blinded them because they thought that made them sing better, and kept them in tiny cages for the rest of their lives.

Falconers don't do that. They either steal the eggs and hatch and rear them at home, or ring the young, in their nests, at a few days old, leave them to be reared and take them just before they can fly. They don't blind them, like larks of old, or keep them in tiny cages. They tie them by their legs, to blocks with leather straps, or 'jesses'.

The registration system has proved a farce and at least seventy-two nests of peregrine falcons have been robbed this year. The Nature Conservancy Council is too wet to speak up and the Department of the Environment, which is responsible for enforcement, appears not to give a damn. The Royal Society for the Protection of Birds, which does care and could help, has had its offers to help police and check registrations and nests spurned by the Department of the Environment.

It seems that nothing can shake the Department out of its lethargy but pressure of public opinion.

34. Rain, Sweet Rain!

Holiday-makers and prissy weathermen were belly-aching at the weekend that the 'nice' weather had come to an end by the middle of September and that we were in for a spell of 'nasty' rain. I was delighted – and so were the deer in the wood. The long, dry summer had parched the countryside and gorgeous, sun-tanned wenches are no compensation, in my eyes, for withering trees that may never recover.

The last drought we had, in 1976, caused damage that didn't show up for several years. Many silver birches in our wood seemed fine the following year, but shrivelled the next. This year, a great and noble beech tree at the top of the woodland ride opposite the house is showing bare twigs at the crown, as ugly as a punk hairstyle. Examining them through field glasses, I have come to the conclusion that the great tree is parched beyond recovery and that recent rains have come too late. By this time next year, I reckon, we shall be forced to fell it and chop it into logs.

A whole stand of aspen trees has gone the same way so that their greyish leaves, that shiver in the slightest breeze, are so brittle that the raindrops knocked them off as lethally as if they had been struck by blasts from a shotgun. Foresters might say that this is a small loss, because aspens have scant commercial value, but I like them because they are the favourite food of caterpillars that would have grown into butterflies and moths to fill my eyes with delight.

So, although human sun-worshippers may mourn the loss of what they may regard as an old-fashioned summer, I was glad to see the rain. I went out in the wood and let it wash over my face, revelling in its purity, and when I returned, the paddock by the window had shed its withered, yellow hue and donned a greener colour. It was quite obvious that this must either have been wishful thinking or an optical illusion, because it was clearly impossible for the colour of the

89

grass to change dramatically in so short a time. I suppose that the explanation was that the prolonged drought had made the grass so brittle that it had become coated with a layer of yellow dust that was washed off and cleansed by the first rain shower. It certainly looked greener – and it must have tasted sweeter, too, because by the time I got back from the wood the deer had come out of cover and were gorging as if they hadn't eaten for weeks. In a way, I suppose, they hadn't, because none of us eats more than we need to subdue the pangs of hunger if we can't stand the food on offer. So for weeks they had picked and finicked, eating the minimum, as I did when confronted by unappetising stodge at school.

Now that several days have passed, the roots are giving thanks for their much longed-for drink by sending up tender shoots as delicate as in spring. Deer can graze longer, because chewing their cud is less arduous than grinding food as brittle as hay, so that they are cramming themselves with delicacies. A fringe benefit is that the joint between the leaves and twigs of trees has weakened prematurely and heavy raindrops send drifts of them fluttering to the ground without waiting for the traditional transition of autumn colours. The green carpet they make does not lie long because deer love browsing as well as grazing and nip off what leaves they can reach. Leaves landing, green, on the ground is an unforeseen labour-saving bonus: the deer are stuffing themselves with leaves as well as new-grown grass.

We have had an added bonus, too. I never believed the story that mushrooms mature overnight, but when my wife and I took the dogs for a walk across familiar clearings, we picked a feed of mushrooms that seemed to arrive by magic. And there is nothing nicer than fresh-picked mushrooms fried with home-cured bacon.

Autumn isn't the end of the year for me; it is the beginning. It is the peak of last year's crops, both wild and cultivated, and the beginning of next. From now on, there will be colours more beautiful than in any foreign land, with a climax when trees are bare and coated with frost. Soft autumn rains are not to be despised.

35. Let Cities Build in Their Green Belts

The House Builders' Federation has started a hare that I predict will still be running when mortal hares are dead. It wants the planners to release more land for building on the fringes of Green Belts round our major towns and cities. Patrick Jenkin, the Environment Secretary, is apparently not too averse to the idea, because he has at least issued a circular to local authorities to ask them to review the tight boundaries that have cocooned cities for many years. As it would be difficult to draw them tighter, the assumption is that the government would like them relaxed.

The conservationists are unfurling their banners, brushing up their woolly hats, and getting ready for the demos. Their lordships in the House of Lords are girding up their loins for battle.

I would be among the last to advocate Green Belt destruction. But attempts to play Canute and to try to turn back the tide of housing expansion is simply to camouflage the symptoms without curing the disease. The harsh fact is that our population is rising and we are aggravating matters by our sloppy policy of letting more folk in from overseas, all of whom have to be housed. So, whatever we say about the Green Belt, houses have to be built somewhere. Nobody bleats louder about the scarcity of houses than the very people who are squealing that the wolves are about to devour the Green Belt.

Strangers can motor across cities from one side to the other, and the ribbon development will give the impression that the whole area is carpeted from edge to edge with houses, factories and shops. But if they flew over the same area, they would be astonished to see that the continuous streets are interspersed with a mosaic of green spaces and waste ground that is neither used nor built over.

Incompetent planners in the past have wasted a vast proportion of the land that could fill much of the needs of the present. They could, at least, have put off the evil day of decisions that are now about to provide a field day for the stirrers-up of trouble.

The mess that planners have made in the countryside is even worse. If the vested interests guarding the sanctity of Green Belts get their way, it is inevitable that the pressure for building land will simply be transferred to quiet places, where there are less voters to defend it.

The point is made by any pretty village. The planners have tried to preserve 'ye olde' features by declaring 'conservation areas', in which planning consent is withheld for any structural alteration that can be seen from the outside. So long as some Rip Van Winkle, from generations past, could come back and walk down the village street without thinking he had landed on Mars, the men from the town hall are smug and self-satisfied. But you can't embalm the countryside like a fossil in a dusty museum because, thank God, the country isn't dead. Any living thing will have changed in the past, will be changing now, and will go on changing in the future. The job of planners is to incorporate such changes, not to sweep them under the carpet, as closer inspection will demonstrate has happened in all their 'conservation' villages.

Behind the façade of the preserved main street, there will be a rash of nasty little jerry-built boxes that have made a bomb for the local spec. builder. In common with so much of our throwaway society, these modern houses are not built to last. Their owners are often part of a shifting society, flitting from job to job in order to win promotion. They are accustomed to a highly competitive way of life, so they regard villagers – whose families have been there for generations – as underprivileged swede-gnawing yokels. Villages are seen as a sort of rural Third World, totally devoid of the blessings of modern civilisation like street lights and public loos, and sports complexes with squash courts and hockey pitches.

One of the changes we could do without in the country is losing the family spirit of traditional small communities as the price we pay for retaining an 'olde' false front to mask the modern rubbish behind. So let the builders have a go at all the spaces left in towns before they are turned loose on either Green Belts or defenceless villages, while planners should concentrate their minds on plans for the future that will stand less chance of ruining either.

36. An Open Letter to the Minister of Agriculture: How Many More Badgers Must Die in Vain?

Dear Michael Jopling,

On behalf of thousands of humane countrymen, I am asking you to examine the policy of your officials towards badgers, while you are still fresh enough in your Ministerial chair to view the subject with an open mind.

The seventh report by the Ministry of Agriculture, under the title 'Bovine Tuberculosis in Badgers', is a catalogue of callous incompetence. It admits that, in spite of all efforts to exterminate badgers in areas where Bovine TB is rife, Ministry action is totally ineffective. The number of annual outbreaks in cattle in controlled areas, since 1976, has averaged 69. In the last three years, there have been 72, 86 and 70. In Avon and parts of Gloucestershire and Wiltshire, the worst-hit areas in the country, new outbreaks since 1976 have averaged 34.8. In the last three years there have been 35, 38 and 36, all worse than average. So, whatever the cause of the spread of TB in cattle may be, the harsh fact is that your officials have been ineffective in combating it, in spite of exterminating upwards of 15,000 (possibly innocent) badgers and squandering up to a million pounds of taxpayers' money. The time has surely come to rethink the whole obscene exercise.

I trust that you took no offence when I pointed out that your officials are callous as well as incompetent. My reason is that, between 1975 and 1982, Ministry ratcatchers were diverted to exterminate badgers by pumping poisonous cyanide gas down their setts. Public concern was so deep that your predecessor, Peter Walker, commissioned an 'independent' report, by his friend Solly Zuckerman, an ageing scientist who had a reputation of being politically astute back in Winston Churchill's time. Whatever Zuckerman's intentions, the report was widely regarded as being a whitewashing exercise to justify the actions of Ministry bureaucrats. But he did recommend that the Chemical Defence Department, who are responsible for germ warfare at Porton Down, should advise on improved techniques for gassing. The report backfired because when the scientists at Porton Down set about this grisly task, the first thing they did was to gas some badgers, using Ministry techniques, to establish what they were expected to prove. Some of the badgers took twenty-five minutes to die an agonising death. The men from Porton Down (not known for being sentimental) were so horrified that they recommended that the practice cease and a more humane death be devised.

Your predecessor, Peter Walker, was forced to execute a humiliating U-turn, wipe the egg off his face and ban badger-gassing by his officials. I gather from colleagues at his Press conference that he was furious at being so let down by people he had supported loyally.

In your latest report, your officials try to implicate the members of the Badger Consultative Panel who, they say, 'agreed unanimously', though they are mainly laymen, ranging from trades union officials, country landowners and National Farmers' Union reps to self-styled eminent authorities on badgers. Hiding behind their skirts is no substitute for testing the gas, which competent scientists would have done seven years before, thereby saving tens of thousands of animals dying in agony.

The alternative decided upon is just as bad if not controlled. With cynical hypocrisy, the Ministry describes it as 'humane control by live trapping'. Unwary badgers are caught in baited cage traps and shot. Others are still strangled in wire nooses, though your officials gloss over that. Last spring your men were trying to eradicate badgers near Leek, in Staffordshire, which is not even listed as one of your control areas. I pointed out that catching sow badgers in spring would leave their unweaned cubs to starve, so, when the glare of publicity was directed on them, they promised that trapping would be suspended till the end of May, when cubs would be weaned. The fact that this

A large, healthy boar badger

even had to be raised with them is some measure of their incompetence as naturalists. Without any announcement, the order was rescinded to the end of April, the Consultative Panel being blamed again, on the grounds that, if not weaned, cubs would be active enough to come above ground when starving, so that they could be killed. But cubs weakened by starvation would be impossible to locate and despatch humanely so the decision to trap sows in milk was indefensible.

Your disgruntled Ministry field workers have told me that decisions are now taken on a political rather than scientific basis. I was told that a vet in the Bristol area reported a post mortem on a sow badger as 'TB free. Placental scars showed she had cubbed. As she was still lactating when killed, the cubs presumably starved.' If, Minister, you think I am exaggerating, you might find it worthwhile to check this report. I shall be interested to hear how you justify it.

Although it has been shown that both badgers and cattle are susceptible to Bovine TB and that it can be passed between them under laboratory conditions, evidence that it is passed in the field is purely circumstantial. Your report repeatedly states 'attributed' cause is badgers, 'thought' to be badger origin, etc. Never proved!

Giving your officials the benefit of the doubt, the fact remains that their remedy is totally ineffective, possibly because clearing any area of badgers simply causes uncontrolled population movement as it is recolonised; often from infected to 'clean' areas. If badgers near infected cattle were immunised, they would be harmless and they would prevent infected badgers entering the area. Specialists in human TB tell me that, although an oral vaccine would be difficult to produce, there is no reason why cage-trapped badgers could not be injected and released, in a harmless state, instead of exterminated to make room for suspects to replace them.

Your government preaches the doctrine of public spending cuts. May I suggest that you dispense with the expensive failures in your Ministry, before they let you down as they did your predecessor. A brand new team, with more constructive ideas, would have a better chance of cracking the problem.

Yours sincerely,

Phil Drabble

21 October 1983

37. Delightful Old Timers

Harry Kelsey would stand head and shoulders above the crowd in the future, as he has for so long in the past. He is not a tall man, physically, but he has a mighty dominant mind. I had the pleasure of sitting next to him at the Fillongley Agricultural Society's annual dinner. Fillongley is a village lost in the limbo between Coventry and Brum, so it is not the area where strangers might expect to find a thriving agricultural community. But it is one of the few such societies which can run a successful one-day show, and the table, groaning under the weight of silver cups to be distributed after dinner, bore witness to the success of such a venture.

The members obviously cared more for the quality of their corn and turnips, beef cattle and randy rams than for the suburban pleasures of pony jumping. Harry Kelsey is president of the society and has breathed fire and enthusiasm into it for sixty years. He is a founder member and he helped put on the first one-day show as long ago as 1913. He and his father and grandfather farmed there, in generations past. His sons and grandsons farm there now. Although it would be easy to mistake him for sixty, he's ninety-six years old. But he made a first-class speech and ate as heartily as any competitor who still uses horses in a ploughing match.

I asked him to tell me the secret of living so long, for I thought it might be useful. His eyes twinkled as he said that it was *not* due to a blameless life! Then, more seriously, he said that friends often asked him why he did not get married again. 'I drew the ace of trumps last time,' he said, 'I might draw the deuce next.'

As a long-serving churchwarden, he detests trendy parsons, who destroy the noble language and tradition of services that have provided security and continuity in our shifting times, striving always to be different because they are incapable of being better. He told me of battles he'd had on the council and the changes he'd seen in farming during a life that had spanned almost a full century.

He introduced me to a friend, who was *only* ninety-two! I had a splendid evening. Such characters are supposed to be extinct, but I reckon that there have never been many – or they wouldn't have rated as characters. If, by some Scargillian twist, we were all brought down to equality today, some would be more equal than others tomorrow. I should try myself. Chaps like Harry Kelsey would always stand out and it has been among my greatest pleasures to rub shoulders with quite a few of them.

Joe Mallen, immortal to all lovers of Staffordshire bull terriers, was a Black Country chainsmith of the old school, who took the greatest pride in forging huge chains, with links weighing five or six hundredweights apiece, to anchor liners like the *Queen Mary*. He would dip his finger into his beer and trace, on the top of the pub table, the precise procedure necessary to turn an impersonal hunk of steel into a masterpiece of quality. 'Times was bad, when I was young,' he said. 'When me and our Lil was going up the aisle, to get wed, I said, "How much money have you got, Lil?" "'Arf a crown, Joe," she said. "Chuck it away, then. Let's start level!"' Joe advised.

Joe's pal Bill always shot with the Earl of Dudley. It was somewhat unconventional shooting, because Bill did not use a shotgun as the real toffs did. Bill used a catapult, which he called a flirter, and he shot at unconventional times, to make things more complicated. 'I likes to get my pheasants against the moon,' he said. 'They look grand, in silhouette.' Indeed, Bill's methods and times were so unconventional that conventional policemen would have described them as poaching, on their charge sheets, if they'd ever caught him. But they didn't catch him, for the simple reason that he never came home carrying any incriminating evidence. His wife, an exceptionally respectable old lady, would take the baby for a walk in the country in his pram next morning. And, when she returned, the pram was stuffed with the pheasants Bill had left concealed. Bill loved Lord Dudley. He said he'd shot with him for twenty years 'but his lordship never found out'.

38. War of the Beetles

Boffins in biology labs often try to blind us with science. If I saw *Rhizophagus grandis* on the guest list of a Christmas party, I should stay away. This would be a great pity because the toffee-nosed name has been dreamed up by some status-conscious biologist, thirsting for academic immortality. He might just as well have called him humble R.G. and introduced him as a fascinating beetle who is set to bring the price of Christmas trees within reach of ordinary folk.

The trouble started when silly bureaucrats sanctioned imports of spruce trees from foreign countries where trees are the victims of a nasty disease caused by a beetle with another high-falutin' name. *Dendroctonus micans* – the Great Spruce Bark Beetle to you and me – was first found in Britain a year last August, when foresters noticed that trees in Mortimer Forest, near Ludlow, in Shropshire, were dying. The reason turned out to be that Spruce Bark Beetles had got under the bark of affected trees and laid eggs which had hatched into maggots. These feed on the wood below the bark and, if there are enough of them, they encircle the whole tree, which yellows and dies. Each beetle can lay between 200 and 300 eggs and the epidemic is thought to have started when diseased trees were imported from France so that adult beetles emerged from them and colonised our trees.

Great Spruce Bark Beetles breed more than seven females to every male, so that their birth rate is predictably high. Although they have wings, they don't fly very much except in the warm months of late summer.

Infection may be localised, but the rates are often astronomic. Foresters in this country rely on what they term good hygiene to prevent the spread of diseases caused by beetles that burrow under the bark of trees. As soon as trees are felled, they are put through a sort of

99

Dendroctonus micans is particularly keen on Norway and Sitka spruce, although it only attacks mature trees

peeling machine that strips the bark and exposes the wood beneath. The bark is destroyed before the beetles have time to develop and attack other trees, so that disease is kept under reasonable control.

When pests are introduced from foreign countries, they are often far more difficult to control because they have no natural enemies. Grey squirrels in this country and rabbits in Australia are obvious examples. The instinct of the sort of boffins who dream up names like *Dendroctonus micans*, instead of plain Spruce Bark Beetle, is always to fall back on science. They concoct satanic brews of poisonous chemicals, which they spray over affected areas – oblivious of the fact that they may exterminate friends as well as foes.

Every year, the Ministry of Agriculture publishes an obscene little book under the title *Approved Products for Farmers and Growers*. It is a catalogue of death because some of the products the Ministry 'approves' are so lethal that they have to warn farmers to keep stock from sprayed areas for up to eight weeks. The authors are too callous to bother how wildlife is to be protected.

The Forestry Commission is not so irresponsible. Research on the reasons that the bark beetle did not do such serious damage in its native land as it appeared to do here disclosed that another beetle preyed upon it. It is the old story that 'Big fleas have little fleas upon their backs, to bite 'em. Little fleas have lesser fleas – and so *ad infinitum*.' They discovered that *Rhizophagus grandis*, to whom I introduced you as R.G., is a natural predator of Spruce Bark Beetles, which are its exclusive diet. It locates broods of the pests and lays its own eggs among them. When the R.G. larvae hatch out, they gobble up the grubs of their prey, without any necessity for spreading dangerous chemicals.

So the Commission has started a breeding colony of R.G.s at Ludlow and it plans to set the progeny free to destroy the pests. It is a far-sighted experiment in biological control and, if the Ministry of Agriculture can be forced to follow such shining examples, England will be a safer place for our descendants to live in.

39. *Unconventional Billy Goat*

It has been possible to appreciate, this week, precisely what the Yankees mean by their expression 'the fall'. The leaves in our oak wood have cascaded down in such torrents that walking along the woodland rides produces sibilant background rustles that drown out all other sounds.

Two weeks ago, the autumn tints were delicate blends of gold and orange and dull greens, that would set sentimental poets off in full spate. The recent frosts and contrasting warm rains scattered the leaves like chaff in a whirlwind. Green rides suddenly turned to gold and so did my animal enclosures. They looked very pretty – but deer and geese don't graze on dead leaves. They need green, succulent grass. So, every autumn, we have to clear the feed paddocks of their blanket of oak leaves to expose the grass which would otherwise die.

Time was when we sweated through the task with a hay rake and brush and aching muscles. The work was boring and heavy when I did it myself – and too expensive when I paid other people. There is now an efficient machine on the market designed specifically for the task. It works like an outsize vacuum cleaner, with a very powerful fan that sucks leaves and other debris into a huge bag that holds more than a couple of sacks of corn. The petrol engine is as powerful as a large mowing machine so that, when it is pushed along at walking pace, the leaves are sucked into its bulging bag as effectively as if a magic wand was waved.

Mechanically-minded youngsters (of all ages!) love it, so there is no difficulty about finding operators positively queueing up – but it was rather pricey. For this reason, it appeared among the list of expenses my accountant demands to prove the cost of keeping the animals I write about for my living.

Weeks later, right out of the blue, the man of figures rang up with a list of queries before he drew up the balance sheet. No one would suggest he is steeped in rural lore. I can never imagine him getting much mud on his boots, because he sits, like a spider waiting for flies, thirteen floors up in a skyscraper office in the heart of the city. 'I'm checking your accounts,' he said, 'and I can't make out what you bought this goat for.' Nor could I, because I had a bellyful of them when we discovered the cottage we'd bought had a herd of historic goats. Nothing would induce me to part with my hard-earned cash to buy a goat that would wreak more havoc than a swarm of locusts. I said I had never bought a goat. I can't stand the brutes.

Nothing arouses deeper suspicions in sharp accountants' minds than clients who waffle around and can't explain expenses they've submitted. 'Come off it,' he said. 'This was a very expensive goat, you can't possibly have forgotten buying it.' The implication was that I was pulling a fast one – and good accountants are as sharp as the taxmen, from whom they are supposed to defend clients, if they get the faintest whiff of a fiddle.

It was my turn to be nettled. I demanded, stiffly, to be given details of the purchase I was alleged to have made. He read it out in all its gory details. It was invoiced as a Billy Goat – and it had cost a lot of money, and now I remembered it quite clearly. Billy Goat, you see, is the trade-name for the mechanical leaf sweeper that wolfs the fallen leaves up faster than they fall. The inventor, I suppose, had been a true countryman who, like me, had been impressed by the insatiable appetite of real goats, which grind up grass and leaves, weeds and treasured garden plants and whatever else is put before them.

The mechanical monster he devised is just as efficient at removing leaves and other debris, but far less destructive because the leaves it munches are ground fine and deposited, from the collecting bag, in perfect condition to make incomparable leafmould for the garden.

The man of figures eventually conceded that we had got our Billy Goat lines crossed and that mine was justified. The perfect conversation-stopper, ever since, has been 'Billy Goat to you, sir!'

40. The Simple Life

One of the joys, as well as the snags, about keeping livestock is that there always has to be someone there to minister to its needs. Poultry has to be fed, water has to be replaced and the dogs have to go out for exercise. There is every excuse to stay at home. I put such responsibilities in the credit column because they mean that I shall be at home for Christmas though strangers might think that I am the father-and-mother of all Scrooges.

When others are sleeping off the effects of their mammoth hangovers, I shall be flying the pigeons or collecting the eggs or going for a walk with the dogs somewhere in the wood. While others cheat the breathalyser in the small hours of the morning, I shall be tucked up in bed, far from coppers and funny party hats. I shall eat a breakfast of home-fed, fat bacon and new-laid eggs. And for Christmas dinner we are going to try one of the geese which were reared on our pool by the wild Canada geese, for whose eggs I substituted a clutch laid by domestic geese. The few relatives and close friends who share our quiet pleasures will be all the company we need and no stranger will darken our portals.

Never having been away from home for Christmas, I confess that I am scarcely qualified to pass judgment on the joys of others. But I can think of nothing which would make me blow my top more quickly than some red-nosed 'life and soul of the party' prodding me in the ribs to join in some hearty party game with strangers with whom I had nothing in common. The idea of the jazzed-up jollity of festivities in some seaside hotel leaves me as cold as a soggy dishcloth. Being overcharged in luxury hotels for grub that is no better and no worse than the nosh dished up in every similar establishment is not to my taste.

Midnight service, with modern jargon that has replaced traditional

Tarka views the world outside

language hallowed by centuries, is commercialised religion by my book. And trendy little parsons, trying to be different because they are incapable of being better, are not on my wavelength.

But the fact that we do not intend to live it up in the conventional sense does not imply that we shan't enjoy ourselves in our own quiet way. Tarka, my Rottweiler bitch, is just beginning to enjoy tracking. So, after Christmas dinner, I shall set off for a walk in the wood, leaving the bitch to champ and fret at the window when she sees me going off without her. It is a good-natured deception because, when I have disappeared from sight for a few minutes, my wife will open the sliding window telling her to 'find the boss'. She will gallop as fast as she can to the point where she saw me disappear into the trees and then she will put her nose to the ground and hunt me as eagerly as a hound hunts a fox. But instead of eating me up when she catches me, she will overwhelm me with affection and we shall both behave as if we were the presidents of some mutual admiration society. And when my wife and our guests, who will follow with Belle the Alsatian, catch up we shall be as pleased to see each other as if we had just returned from space.

I have put fresh litter on the floor of the fowlpen so that when the weather is bad the hens can stay indoors and scratch for goodies hidden in sweet, dry straw. It may sound a very simple pleasure, but every true stockman has shared the delight of watching the stock he cares for revelling in the conditions he supplies. It is something that men can never know who cram seven birds into a tiny battery cage.

The first catch of wintry sun will spark off the blackbirds into rehearsal for their mating song of spring – and there is no music, composed and played by man or sung by foreign birds, that can hold a candle to a blackbird's song.

Our wood is rather special, too. Herons are early nesting birds and we always reckon to see the first of the season prospecting for a nesting site at about this time of year. It may be Christmas Eve or Boxing Day or Christmas Day itself. Sometime over the period, our herons will return, and to welcome them is a pleasure that money couldn't buy.

So may I wish you a Christmas as simple and happy as mine!

41. Lights That Put Bill in Panic

It came as quite a shock when I was looking up something in an old diary to discover that the first broadcast I did was on steam radio in April 1947. And I've been messing about on the wireless ever since, a small matter of thirty-seven years in April, if I am still alive and well by then.

Spurred into reminiscence, I find that my first appearance on the telly was in 1952. Not, perhaps, of much interest to anyone else, but I particularly remember that first time on the box because my tame badger bit me! Godfrey Baseley had invited me to take part in a children's programme from Rodbaston, the Staffordshire Farm Institute. 'What can you bring?' he asked. Apart from my dog, who would have behaved impeccably, there wasn't much but domestic hens or ferrets or similar run-of-the-mill creatures. 'But I thought you'd got a tame badger,' he said. 'Can't you bring that?' I'm not the chap to chuck away opportunities for simple reasons, like impracticality. So I accepted with well-feigned confidence.

The badger I had was Bloody Bill Brock, my first and only badger in confinement. I had got him as a cub, which would be illegal now, and reared him on the bottle. Almost any young creature that you rear on the bottle becomes 'fixated' on you. He literally believes that you are his mother. So Bloody Bill had grown up with utter confidence in me and he treated me as if I really was his mum. He played like a pup, though a very rough pup indeed. Badgers have exceptionally thick and tough skin, which is practically untearable. They also seem impervious to pain.

I was less thick-skinned. After most evening sessions of rough and tumble, my hands and wrists were scratched and torn as if I had been catapulted through a hawthorn hedge. But it was all good fun and gave the young animal the exercise and play he needed.

Bloody Bill Brock amusing himself by tugging at the author's trouser
turn-ups!

But by the time Godfrey invited me to take part in his programme,
my badger was practically full-grown. Now, full-grown badgers, even
when they have been bottle-reared, are subject to natural instincts
and fears of the unknown as they grow out of cubhood. As a naturalist, I was well aware that natural caution will make any wild animal
very wary if suddenly confronted by strangers and strange surroundings. And when wild animals like badgers get wary, they also get very
trigger-happy. It is asking for trouble to mess about with them if they
get in a panic.

So I made a large packing case and put it in the loose-box where
Bill spent the day while I was away at work. I filled it with lovely soft
bedding and removed other comfortable litter from the shed. The
idea was that, when the time came to take him to Rodbaston, my
badger would be so used to the packing-case sleeping box that I could
load it (and him!) on to a van and transport him without giving the
impression that he was in a strange place. It worked like a dream.
When they asked me, 'What can he do?' I traded a silly answer for
what I regarded as a silly question. 'He follows at heel, like a spaniel

dog,' I replied, without the glimmer of a smile.

Badgers, you see, are very short-sighted and hate getting lost because a lost badger, in another badger's territory, will get the father-and-mother of good hidings from the resident occupant. So I knew that if I lifted my badger from his box, took him a few yards and put him down, he would follow at my heels, not because I had trained him but simply because I would be the only familiar object, to which he would stick, like glue, for fear of getting lost.

What I didn't know, because I had never seen television from backstage before, is that they have innumerable rehearsals. As there was only live TV in those days they simply had to get it right, because if they had a cock-up, everybody saw it. Bill Brock was fine for the first few rehearsals, but he wasn't in the right union. He got more and more mutinous each time I lifted him from his box. On the last rehearsal, when I bent to lift him, he grabbed my wrist in his jaws that made a vice seem sissy – and wouldn't let go. All the camera saw was my backside instead of me holding a badger.

As it was only a dress rehearsal, the viewers fortunately couldn't hear my language over the microphone! But, as they say, it all came right on the night. I didn't risk lifting him out of his box but started by holding him. When I put him down and went for my walk, he followed closer at heel than the best trained spaniel. I have basked in his reflected glory ever since!

42. *Irresistible Power*

The ancient hawthorn tree on the edge of the paddock rocked as helplessly as a rotten tooth being loosened for extraction by the dentist. It was an eerie sight in the half-light of dawn during the storms of January. This was no example of an irresistible force meeting an immovable object to produce a stalemate. The venerable old tree was on a hiding to nothing. Each time it rocked, the crown of the tree bowed lower until, at last, a horrific, splintering crash split trunk from roots and it measured its length on the ground.

Hours later, the pitiless whine of the chainsaw had reduced it to a welcome pile of logs for winter fuel. The old tree had stood about thirty feet high and was probably a survivor of some forgotten hawthorn hedge which, judging by the size of this relic of the past, had been grubbed out fifty or sixty years ago.

We were very fond of it because, apart from its blossom at Maytime and berries which had fed generations of birds, it had gnarled old branches which made perfect nesting sites for wrens to rear their young. The fact that the branches were bare of leaves, so that they offered minimum resistance to the wind, simply emphasises how ruthless the gale was, so I wandered round, with fingers crossed, to check what further damage it had done.

It is easy to think of winter only in terms of snow and ice and flood, which are tangible and obvious. Wind, as an enemy, tends to be out of mind simply because it is out of sight. Only the results of its spite can be seen. A friend, about ten miles from where I live, has a house in a hollow, at the foot of Cannock Chase. It seems in summertime to be a marvellously sheltered spot, a suntrap that gives illusions of security. Yet, twice in the last year, freak storms have cut a swathe clean through the trees there, as neatly as if done by a mammoth, invisible scythe. Large trees, holly bushes and even small rhododendrons have all been levelled to the ground.

110

Wind damage is equally unpredictable in our wood. When the dogs and I wandered round to see what fellow casualties had joined the old hawthorn, we found remarkably few. Three old birch trees had bitten the dust, but birches have short lives and their successors grow quickly to replace them. Though birch logs do not burn as hot as hawthorn, they burn bright and will be a welcome addition to the log shed.

The most astonishing casualty was a young pine tree, only twenty years old and standing amidst a large plantation of trees exactly similar in size. None but this one had been touched. But, for no apparent reason, this single tree, healthy and supple so far as I could see, had split off about fifteen feet from the crown. It hadn't just broken the top off – the severed piece was in three separate parts, splintered to smithereens at the break points, for all the world as if the wind had cracked it, like a whip, until it had literally exploded into pieces.

I puzzled about how and why this particular tree had been selected but could make neither head nor tail of it. The deer are more clever than that! They hate high winds more than any other type of storm, perhaps because the roar of tempest drowns out the sound of enemies approaching. They seem to disappear off the face of the earth when gales are howling through the trees.

When high winds are impeded by solid objects, such as walls, the air spills over the wall, somersaulting away in uncontrollable eddies that are no less destructive than a solid sheet of wind. But, when the wind blows through trees, it slows down like gravy through a sieve. The sound peters out and there are odd hollows in our wood that are as peaceful and silent in storm-force winds as at the height of summer. That is where the deer hide out till calm reigns again. They are warm and the air is quiet enough for them to hear the approach of foes. They know, by instinct, where they are least likely to be crushed by a storm-felled tree. We have much to learn from them!

43. *Hard Times on the Farm*

A favourite missile in the modern sport of 'farmer-bashing' is the subject of factory farming. Pressure groups explode with the idea of seven laying hens crammed into a cage too small for a canary. The tender-hearted wilt at visions of pigs in sweat boxes, where temperatures are uncomfortably high, daylight is excluded, and life is so boring that there is nothing to do but bite off each other's tails.

But times are improving for farm stock, whatever the Orwellian predictions for the human race. This is partly due to sales resistance generated by opponents of unacceptable modern methods – and partly because techniques of farming seem as susceptible to fashion as women's clothes or hairstyles. The first forced change was probably in methods of rearing calves for veal. For some years it had been found to be profitable to confine calves to individual crates, as narrow as coffins, and to feed them on a diet from which iron had been excluded to make them anaemic, so that their flesh would be white. When the method was widely publicised, the public was so disgusted that many people refused to eat veal and the bottom fell out of the market. Some calves are still reared under these disgraceful conditions but the largest producers of veal have got the message and keep them in strawed yards where they have company and comfort and a more natural diet.

So many customers have been put off eggs produced in battery cages where hens are on diets designed to make the yolks look golden, however rubbery they taste, that there is now a market for higher-priced eggs laid by hens that can move freely on deep litter or on free range.

When Big Business discovers that there is money in humane stockmanship, Big Business grows civilised, too! Spotlights on unacceptable practices produce results when the spotlighters are willing to put their money where their consciences are.

But fashion has its influence too. The boffins in agricultural research establishments are always looking for fresh ideas which are sometimes better but, too often, only different. Researchers can only get higher qualifications, such as doctorates of philosophy, by doing original research.

Many big-business farmers regard pigs or poultry or other stock simply as impersonal items on their balance sheets. Cocooned in their offices, they are so far removed from reality that they never smell the horror of a battery house or soil their hands by mucking out a pigsty. So they fall for the blandishments of their scientific advisers and tie their cash up in intensive husbandry – until they discover that unnaturally-kept stock is susceptible to an unnatural amount of disease, and an unacceptable level of sales resistance.

So, the pendulum swings. Progressive farmers are now rearing pigs in huts on open fields, where the sows and piglets are free to range over several acres, grubbing up the soil with their powerful snouts for food, as Nature intended they should. They may not be quite as profitable as factory-reared pigs – but losses from disease are less, and satisfaction from genuine stockmanship is far greater.

But don't be deluded that, because farming was old-fashioned, it was necessarily a bed of roses for farm stock. Sheep, wintering in the wild fells of mountainous country, know a different kind of hardship. At this time of year, whatever the weather in the cosseted lowlands, there are always bulldozers and four-wheel-drive trucks needed to take food to stock, when snowdrifts are too deep for them to find food naturally. In inaccessible hills only the fittest survive.

Working as much with shepherds as I do, I hear scores of tales about the marvellous instinct for survival in the sheep, and of the courage and enterprise of the shepherds and collies that look after them. The sheep seek out the sheltered hollows and cower together in them for mutual warmth. The several feet of drifted snow that often buries them serve as an eiderdown so that slow starvation becomes their worst threat. Clever collies listen and smell and mark them, from the surface, as eagerly as a terrier marking rats, so that the shepherds can dig down to them and rescue them.

Even so, there are often grievous losses in bad winters, so that the

The isolated Gwydir Forest, near Betws-y-coed, Caernarfonshire. Often the only way that precious food supplies can reach the flock is via helicopter drops

modern fashion is to bring the whole flock in before the foul weather, and overwinter them in covered yards. It may cost more at the time, but there will be more wool and mutton on the balance sheet later, and the stock will have had a better life!

44. Bureaucrats Fudge Poison Dangers*

When the Danish trawler *Dana Optima* lost eighty drums of weedkiller overboard in a recent storm, Mr Jopling, Minister of Agriculture, flew post-haste to Denmark, to discuss a plan of action with the Danish Environment Minister. Senior Cabinet Ministers do not panic to that extent unless there is serious risk of some major catastrophe, and the worry was that the drums would split open or corrode, spewing their contents into the sea. This would not only poison fish in the vicinity, but might also poison the people who ate them, so our Minister of Agriculture and his Danish counterpart are to be commended for taking responsible action.

Not so the Minister's subordinates, who made light of the dangers of contaminated fish. 'Because the drums are full, they would sink to the bottom of the sea. And, even if they burst, they would have little effect on fish life,' they said. John MacGregor, a Minister of State, who answered questions in Parliament while the Minister was holding the urgent talks on the crisis with the Danes, said that contaminated fish were unlikely to reach our shores. But he had advised fishermen to avoid the area where the barrels of poison were lost.

Such contradictions would be worrying enough over minor matters, but when the risk of poisoning is enough to send Cabinet Ministers scurrying abroad, it is time to examine the facts.

Dinoseb, the weedkiller contained in the drums, is listed among the products the Ministry of Agriculture *approves* for farmers to use to control weeds in many agricultural crops and is officially listed as poison. It is so dangerous that farmers are warned not to allow animals and poultry to have access to treated areas for at least ten days. No advice is given how to safeguard wildlife, which can't be excluded by fences!

So the Minister appears to have acted more responsibly than his

115

* This article was originally published in February 1984.

subordinates, who played the whole thing down. The attitude of the Ministry of Agriculture to the use of poisons for the control of both animal and insect pests is so alarming that constituents should insist that their MPs enforce proper controls to reduce the use of dangerous poisons.

Lucretia Borgia was the daughter of Alexander VI, a fifteenth-century Pope, who should have been above producing such impious daughters. But Lucretia earned everlasting fame because she not only poisoned most of her family but almost anyone else she didn't like. She would have been quite at home amongst modern agricultural scientists!

I have often criticised the Ministry's *Approved Products for Farmers and Growers* which lists the chemical pesticides to be used against insects and plants that damage crops, because so many birds and beneficial insects are killed as well. The fact that their death is accidental makes it no less final! But government scientists also set out to poison animals and birds deliberately. The poison used to kill rats killed cats and owls and other predators, because the animals dying of poison were obviously the easiest to catch. Rats, being the survivors they are, developed resistance to Warfarin, which was evolved to replace the acute poison used before.

Ministry pest officers use strychnine, one of the most persistent and dangerous poisons known, to kill moles, and less scrupulous people acquire it for moles but use it for crows and foxes and stray dogs.

A secret poison, developed by scientists from the germ warfare department at Porton Down, was tried against foxes at Kirkcudbright a couple of years ago. Persistent rumours suggested that crows dissected the bait – and left the poison for anything else that would eat it. Peggy Fenner, who answered questions in Parliament on behalf of the Ministry, admitted the trials were held and, on December 1, 1982, announced: 'The results of the trial are currently being assessed.' We are still waiting to hear!

On November 30, 1982, the same lady, replying to another question from Ivan Lawrence, MP for Burton-on-Trent, denied that her department was carrying out any field trials using poison bait against rabbits. When I checked with the Ministry press office, I was told that trials had been carried out on *baits*, but not *poison baits* – although poison was being considered as a control! A skilful, if misleading play upon words, which prompted the unworthy thought that a witch-hunt among Ministry personnel might uncover a few potential modern Lucretia Borgias.

45. *Both Sides of the Hedge!*

The Council for the Preservation of Rural England is having another purge on hedge removal which, it claims, destroys the beauty of the countryside. A farmer in Suffolk has grubbed out so many hedges that one field covers 350 acres – about twice the size of many Midland farms.

Whether the views of the CPRE, that such folk are villainous vandals, are right or wrong, such actions are certainly foolish. A newly-ploughed field of more than 300 acres is a 'prairie' of plough by anybody's standards and the great danger is that gut-griping east winds will dry out the soil to fine dust and blow it away like a desert sandstorm. But it is worth looking on both sides of the hedge to see the farmer's point of view as well.

Whatever conservationists think, not all farmers are vandals. They do not just visit the countryside for a stroll on fine Sundays. They love, work, play, eat, drink and sleep in the middle of the countryside. They give several reasons for wanting their fields to be large, by old-fashioned standards, some of which should be accepted by the most rabid conservationists, though some may not.

The most compelling reason is mechanisation. The real reason for our urban unemployment is not so much profit-greedy employers or bloody-minded trades unions, as silicon chips and automation. The same applies to the countryside. We are in the midst of an industrial revolution as severe as the advent of steam with Boulton and Watt. It was long before then that the lovely patchwork pattern of the English countryside was created, by hedges which divided the little fields that horses needed to manoeuvre. When little fields were inched out a bit, to give tractors room to swing in bigger arcs, people complained about so-called 'progress'. Now that the old-fashioned tractors have been scrapped in favour of giants with all the power of bulldozers, the

118

The hedgy landscape of Devon (above), as compared with the geometric prairies of plough in Lincolnshire (below), where hedges have long since disappeared

machines they operate rival the earthmoving machinery developed for airfields in the last war. Such implements resemble the figments of imagination beloved by the writers of space fiction and little fields would fetter them till they couldn't earn their diesel – so hedges have to go.

But there are less logical reasons for carving the countryside into even larger slices. Every yard a hedgerow takes is one yard less of corn, and on a balance sheet is a pound or two of loss when they tot up their dividends. A yard of corn is profit – even if it is only consigned to a 'corn mountain' and sold at a loss to our Communist enemies. So some pull hedges out, not to make room for machines but simply for profit.

Others grudge the shade they spread, which backens plants that need the sun to ripen, while some think they simply harbour pests. 'Pests' are weeds to some and wild flowers to others, and caterpillars may produce beautiful butterflies or be pests that gorge on cabbage.

Hedgerows are breeding habitats for nesting birds – which, in turn, may raid the fruit or eat the pests that rot it. They are the main runs for animals to cross the farm or sanctuary for guzzling rabbits. As with so many controversies about the countryside, there is neither jet black nor pure white, but room for compromise between extremes.

Before William the Conqueror and his Normans came, England was almost completely clothed in woodland. Hunting was more important then than growing corn or feeding cattle. Hedges were planted as the land was cleared for agriculture down the centuries, and now the hedges give way.

Time never stands still in the country, but if we could bang the heads of the two extremes together, those who are prepared to give as well as take could still leave a land which will fill their descendants' eyes with pleasure.

46. *The Joys of Spring*

In the good days, when steam engines kept time on the railways, I was lost in wonderment and awe at the genius of Mr Bradshaw, whose mathematical mind could devise such sophisticated timetables. It was, of course, nothing compared to the electronic computers which spew out a jumble of figures that pretend to predict when modern trains arrive.

But neither human brains nor the wonders of modern science can hold a candle to the simple animals and birds that live in our countryside. How, for example, does the song thrush in your garden decide when it is time to build her nest? The February weather has see-sawed from frost to muggy dampness, back to snow and hoar frost and contradicted itself by dazzling us with deceptive sunshine. If the thrush was conned into building her nest and laying a clutch of eggs a couple of weeks ago, her chicks would have died in the shell or been starved on hatching, because there were no insects to feed them.

Yet Nature's timetable is so synchronised that all the essentials for wildlife to breed slide into place more sweetly than a jigsaw. Our deer, for example, are a pretty dingy lot. The bottom end of February and the beginning of March are the hungriest time of the year. Young grass and leaves are not yet sprouting, to get them in condition and make the blood course round their veins. Last year's grass is tough and dry and withered, about as nourishing as unappetising old-fashioned ship's biscuits. The result is that the deer are thin from cramming themselves with pack-belly that fills but does not fatten. Their coats are harsh and unattractive, but deep down the new coat is beginning to grow, making the old one itch. So, if you walk round our wood, you will see tufts of hair about half as big as an old shaving brush, as if some sadistic vandal had taken handfuls of hair from every deer that passed. That is not the cause of the hairy litter. The tufts of loosening hair drop out when the deer scratch their itching hides with delicate cloven hooves. It is a sign of approaching spring, whatever commonsense and the weathermen say on the wireless. And the old coats, cast off as the deer prepare for their breeding season, are just the material for birds, like blue tits, to use for lining their nests.

In much the same way, the song thrushes and blackbirds start to sing long before it would be prudent to build a nest and lay a clutch of eggs. The hawthorn hedges are now so bare that, if eggs were laid, they would immediately be stolen by magpies or jays or crows. That doesn't stop the songbirds prospecting for the most desirable sites for spring and summer residence of the future. I am the last to suggest that they think, consciously, that when the leaves do clothe the bare branches, this or that fork would be the ideal place to hide a growing brood. But, if they don't indulge in such constructive thought, instinct does the same job for them. When they get the spontaneous gut feeling that they have discovered the perfect site, they sing a song about it.

The boffins assure us that it isn't a song of joy. On the contrary, it is a hymn of hate, claiming sole possession of the territory and warning off all other rivals. By the time they have established their claims, the leaves will be covering the twigs, they will have attracted mates, built their nests and laid their eggs. By the time their eggs are hatched, the next piece of jigsaw will have been slotted in, insects will have come out of hibernation and be a plenteous crop to feed the insatiable fledglings.

By then the deer will have got their summer coats, more russet than the dowdy hues of winter, so that their new colours will blend superbly with the vegetation, dappled by sunlight, and only the jewelled glint of the fawn's eye will give away its hiding place.

The whole complex pattern of life in the wild had been perfected so long before primitive man climbed down from his tree that silicon chips and computers are mere scribble-talk by comparison.

47. Licence to Kill Ten Innocent Birds*

My belief that fools and their money are soon parted was sired by childhood games of put-and-take. Every player took his turn at spinning a little brass top carrying various instructions from 'Put All' or 'Take All', to less dramatic 'Put' or 'Take' one or two or three. We didn't play for money, because we had none. We played for toffees or liquorice allsorts or gobstoppers. Whatever the stake, I always lost. I am not a good loser and those early games of put-and-take cured me of gambling for good.

Put-and-take fishing is different. There is no gamble about it because it is a dead cert, even if an expensive one. The way it operates is that a fishing club or water authority buys young trout from a fish farm and rears them in large tanks, flowing with fresh water. The fish are fed artificially on 'fish pellets', not unlike breakfast cereals, which come in half-hundredweight paper sacks. The moment a handful of pellets hit the surface the fish swirl greedily after them, making the water surface seem to boil.

When they are large enough, say a pound or so in weight, they are set free in the lake or reservoir to amuse the sportsmen, who flick their rods and cast a fly. The poor tame fish, brought up on the kindness of their keeper throwing handfuls of fish pellets, think the fly is another easy meal – so take the bait.

I listened, recently, to the Bishop of Woolwich splitting ecclesiastical hairs about the philosophy of sport. He didn't like fox hunting but he liked fishing because he ate the fish. He couldn't have meant coarse fishing, because the chaps who sit on crates of beer, along the canal, dangling maggots on a hook, put their fish back at the end of their competition. So the bishop must have meant trout or salmon fishing, which is the Top People's sport, a high-powered status symbol.

By my standards, such fish are dear grub. Their flesh is pallid white,

123

* This article was originally published in March 1984.

Coarse fishing in the Thames at Abingdon in Oxfordshire – still the working
man's sport

with a texture like cotton wool, and it costs a mint of money to catch them. The put-and-take fishery at Blithfield Reservoir, near Abbots Bromley, charges members of the fishing club £380 a year for the privilege of taking out what the fish farmers put in. They will put in 33,000 trout, between the weights of one-and-a-quarter and five pounds, between March and September this year. When turned loose, they will be tame enough for novices to catch. Some of the members of the club are anything but that, so the skilled fishermen should have plenty of trophies to boast about.

There is but one tiny snag. Not every fisherman at Blithfield is a bishop or tycoon, though the £380 membership fee must keep the club exclusive! Despite my reluctance to gamble, I will lay a pound to a gooseberry that the most skilled fishermen there wear feathers but pay no subscription.

There have been bitter complaints that too many fish are being caught by cormorants, which are large, black diving birds more often found fishing along the sea coast. Some avian grapevine has told them that the fishing is better at Blithfield. You might think that fishermen as keen as trout anglers might admire the skill of feathered fellow

A cormorant in flight

anglers and be happy to share a little sport. Or, perhaps, that folk who can afford £380 a year for sport could afford to put a few in for the birds. Instead of such charity, they have demanded blood for supper and asked for the cormorants to be shot. As they are protected under the recent Wildlife and Countryside Act, they cannot be shot without a licence from the Ministry of Agriculture, Fisheries and Food, who can issue a licence if there is economic damage to property or crops.

Commonsense would suggest that this was meant to protect crops grown for food, not sport. But the track record of the Ministry with any sort of wildlife is abysmal. When they take an interest in wild creatures it is as good as the kiss of death. They asked the Nature Conservancy Council for their advice about the Blithfield cormorants and the NCC advised against destroying them. But the Ministry of Agriculture still went arrogantly ahead and have issued a licence to shoot ten.

It seems quite wrong that they should be judge and jury. I hope there will be enough public outcry to shift the responsibility for giving licences from the Ministry of Agriculture to the Nature Conservancy Council.

What is the point of spending taxpayers' money on a Nature Conservancy Council that is not allowed to conserve nature?

48. *When a TV Crew Came Close to the Brute Reality*

I was asked, the other day, to do a short film for breakfast television to discourage visitors to the countryside from letting their dogs chase sheep, especially in March and April.

At this time of the year, the fields are stuffed with snowy white woolly lambs which concentrate the public's mind on Mary and her nursery rhyme instead of the exorbitant price of mutton.

It so happens that my neighbour, David, keeps 600 ewes, which are currently suckling over 1,000 lambs. So I wasn't short of raw material. Not, that is, if I could persuade my neighbour to co-operate! Luckily he had never been on the box before, so he didn't know what he was letting himself in for. 'Leading a lamb to the slaughter,' would have been a fair quotation. So David, who manages the farm beyond our wood, was offered the star role and, to clinch the deal, lunch at a local pub with the crew, who came all the way from London to film the epic.

The lunch might have scored one star out of five but the crew's director took our breath away. She was a slip of a girl, just out of university, I should guess, with high heels and a simulated fur coat that reached almost to her ankles. David yards his sheep all winter, and his yards are neat and tidy. But she was pretty lucky she didn't have to wade through the quagmires that are more typical of farms, or her fur coat would have looked as if a pack of hounds had chased her. To give her her due, neither sleet nor rain nor sunshine nor belly-griping wind made the slightest difference to her. She ploughed on through her story as if it had been high summer. In this she was fairly lucky, for she nearly didn't get a story at all, as the alternative would have been blue pencilled because of violence.

As David and I were setting off to meet the crew at the local, we were confronted by a pair of dogs, running along the edge of our wood towards a field where he had 100 ewes and lambs. They were unattended and muddied up to their eyeballs, so that there was no shadow of doubt that they had spent their morning hunting. Whether their quarry had been rabbits, deer or sheep was anybody's guess. But, as a prudent farmer, David's instinct was to tell the film crew to get lost so that he could slip home for his gun to make sure that two unattended, hunting dogs did not run amok among his sheep.

We got out of the car, swearing at the dogs in terms they obviously understood, backing up our threats with showers of brickbats, which made them return whence they'd come, encouraging us to carry on.

The reaction of the crew, when they heard how nearly they had come to having graphic illustrations for the film they'd come to make, was very interesting. Half of them thought that it is quite unjustified to shoot dogs which are worrying stock because the instinct of dogs is to hunt. The other half agreed with me that, although there are no bad dogs, only bad masters, dogs which start to worry sheep enjoy it so much that they are incurable and have to suffer for the stupidity of their owners.

So I started off the film by introducing Tarka, my Rottweiler bitch, to a lamb that was being reared on the bottle. My dogs are completely steady to stock when they are with me, and they never meet stock on their own because they are never allowed to wander by themselves. The best of them will fall for temptation. So Tarka was most intrigued to meet her lamb and licked its mouth which obviously tasted deliciously of its recent feed of milk. Just the sort of shot to make sentimental viewers drool! Then I demonstrated how innocent strangers, with dogs properly controlled on leads, can still disturb stock in fields simply by their presence.

The cruelty of sheep worrying was obvious, but David and I underlined it by explaining that the loss of a ewe and a couple of lambs would set the farmer back £150 or so. Dogs causing a flock of ewes to panic before they lamb, instead of after, can cause even more damage by making them abort. But the worst offenders are not dogs but their owners. Some walk over other people's land without controlling dear Fido. Others turn their pets loose at night or when they go to work. Those that stray into fields with stock are liable to get a one-way ticket. I am sorry for the dogs but it serves their owners right.

49. Three's Company!

Frenchmen boast about bad habits which we would sweep discreetly under the carpet. The French expression '*ménage à trois*' describes the situation where one chap shacks up with two women in the same household, which does not occur in our more civilised society. Or, if it does, we keep quiet about it. Households for three are not our scene. By an odd coincidence, there is a *ménage à trois* outside my study window, though not a human one.

Every spring, a pair of Canada geese settle on our pool and nest on the island. The geese were not always welcome because they brought a flock of friends with them, who scoffed more grass than I could spare and fouled what they did not eat. Last year, I rather turned the tables on them.

The gander is a he-man among geese. He appropriated the island in the middle of the pool to allow his mate to nest in peace, and he literally knocked hell out of all intruders. As a result, we only had one pair, which neither ate too much grass nor fouled what they didn't eat. I was so delighted to have a pair which kept rivals away that I scattered a bowl of wheat for them every morning when I went out to feed the poultry. Although Canada geese are wild birds, they are quick to accept human kindness and soon get as tame as robins. They immediately associated me with food and marched up the paddock to meet me when I went out with my bowl of corn. Being the idle Jack I am, I first met them halfway across the paddock and then put the corn just outside my study window and left them to come and get it. They soon delighted our friends by practically eating out of their hands, but it dawned on me that the goose was laying eggs in the nest on the island which would hatch into a mini-flock that might raise the same problems as their predecessors.

The practical solution was to remove their eggs and replace them by a clutch of eggs from domestic geese. If they hatched these, which

I doubted, at least we would have the consolation of eating the geese which ate our grass! To our great surprise they hatched four domestic goslings from the four eggs we replaced, and one wild gosling of their own from an egg the goose laid after we did the swop. They reared all five, but their own wild gosling deserted them and flew away to join the wild flocks in July, when wild Canada geese gather on reservoirs and lakes.

Our domestic goslings were far too heavy and large to stand any chance of getting airborne, so they were unable to fly. Although they were snowy white and didn't look in the least like Canada geese, their wild foster parents stayed with them for several weeks before instinct triumphed and they went to join the flock.

The arrangement was so satisfactory that I hope to repeat it this year and the first part of the exercise has been executed without a hitch. The eggs have been changed, the goose is incubating them, under the delusion that they are the ones she laid. And the gander is standing guard. Or, to be more precise, he was standing guard.

Primrose Dell, at the far end of the wood, has a much smaller pool without an island, so I was very surprised to see another pair nest there. The goose made a shallow scrape and started to lay an egg a day. When she had laid them, she covered them carefully with wisps of dry grass, which formed a perfect camouflage. Even the sharp-eyed crows failed to find them, though the shells were so thick that they might have defeated their chisel-like bills if they had. It was never put to the test because, when the daily increase in the clutch had reached five eggs – they disappeared overnight. Crows didn't have them because there would have been telltale splinters of shell, as clues.

I'm pretty certain that the thieves were not human crows either, because there were no strange footprints in the mud, and the reputation of Tarka, my Rottweiler guard dog, does nothing to encourage trespassers. Although the eggs were so well hidden, a light blanket of grass does not imprison scent. I reckon that the culprit was a prowling fox which got an appetising whiff in passing, though I should love to know how he shattered the smooth shells to reach the luscious contents.

There could only be an open verdict at the inquest, but the drama

Surrogate parenthood!

did not finish with robbery. The pair of geese that had nested down at Primrose Dell deserted, came up to the big pool by the house, and tried to nest on the island, where the goose was already sitting on my domestic eggs. Our gander was not standing for any such nonsense. He attacked the strange gander so viciously that he flew away to safer parts. The strange goose was overcome by the masculine virility of our gander, who had so little trouble in seeing off her mate. He obviously turned her on till she, in turn, was irresistible.

It must be very boring to sit around, twiddling your webbed feet for a solid month while your mate is unattainable, sitting on dull eggs whatever advances you make. Husbands know the feeling with over-domesticated wives.

So the strange goose and our gander are inseparable and the aston-ishing thing is that the dutiful old spouse, sitting on her eggs, seems to have taken no offence. When she comes off to feed, she joins the other two as if the interloper was her closest friend. They are a *ménage à trois*!

Perhaps Canada geese came originally from that part of the continent where French Canadians live?

50. *Foxy Squatters in the Warren*

About six weeks ago, I noticed that a very large rabbit bury had been opened up by foxes. There is nothing very unusual about that because young rabbits are a staple item in the diet of foxes in spring. Doe rabbits normally have their young in a single hole or 'stop' where they make a nest of dry grass, lined with soft fur plucked from their own tummies. These stops may either be single passages in a large warren or, more often, single tunnels in a bank or under a tree root a hundred yards or more away from the main colony.

The young rabbit kittens are left alone in the nest except when the doe calls to suckle them two or three times a day. I imagine that they begin to squeak when they grow hungry so that any passing fox or badger hears them. Or they may smell strong enough to give away their hiding place. When this happens, the fox enlarges the hole, scoops the nest out onto the surface and eats her prey so that, when next I pass by, the scooped-out hole and defiled bedding are all the clues I need to know about the drama.

Opening up a large warren is slightly different. More than one tunnel is usually enlarged and close examination reveals the unmistakable footprints of regular use by foxes. The prints are tighter and neater than would be left by dogs but they could be mistaken for a large cat. The purpose of this exercise is not to plunder a litter of rabbits but to enlarge their warren enough to provide permanent accommodation for a vixen and her cubs. She usually opens up several possible desirable residences and makes her final choice at the last minute.

I started watching the warren where I thought she had produced her litter about an hour before dusk, several weeks ago, picking a tree stump eighty yards away to sit on. On the very first night, she appeared at the mouth of the hole at half-past seven exactly. A black

A young fox cub dreams of future mischief

nose and white chin poked cautiously out to test the breeze. When she thought there were no enemies about she climbed out and sat, motionless, at the edge of the hole for a quarter of an hour or so.

I was most surprised by the rabbits' reaction. They continued to share most of the warren and sat completely devoid of fear within five yards of their traditional enemy. This fascinated me so much that I have been back almost every night for the last six weeks.

Although her behaviour suggested that she had cubbed, I saw no

sign of her young until last Saturday night. The evenings have leng-
thened since I first saw her, and she has been coming out about half
an hour before dusk and setting off to hunt about half-past eight.

Young puppies cause their dams a lot of discomfort by scratching
their udders with needle-sharp claws to make the milk flow freely. I
reckon the vixen has been suffering the same because she has now left
her cubs to lie-up in another part of the warren. The rabbits seem
totally unafraid and one old warrior sits fearlessly within a yard of
the cubs' entrance, ears cocked like radar scanners, obviously listening
to sounds underground.

The cubs are doubtless growing hungry, but they never even peep
out until their dam surfaces and comes to sit outside their hole. When
she arrives, the sentry rabbit hops casually away, not in the least
afraid, and she, in turn, ignores him. I am not, of course, near enough
to hear what sound she makes but, as soon as she arrives, the cubs
rush out and tumble over each other to get at the milk bar.

The warren faces due west and, during the recent dry spell, has
been floodlit by the setting sun, in which the vixen basks while her
cubs play more prettily than the most delightful human ballet. After
half an hour or so, the vixen stretches and yawns – and her cubs
disappear below ground as if by magic. I cannot make out how she
communicates with them, but her discipline is iron hard. When she
goes off hunting, they never show another whisker!

Nor do I know how the rabbits know she is harmless, because food
remains prove that the main diet of the litter – is rabbit! An old
country belief is that foxes never take poultry or game near their own
earth.

I shall keep watching till she takes her cubs away, but I have a
shrewd suspicion that when their appetites grow hard to satisfy, they
may discover to their cost the worth of old wives' tales. Perhaps
cunning foxes make provision for hard times by using local warrens
as a larder to be raided only when their cubs need emergency rations!

51. The Parson's Rook

When I was young, I was always invited to go rook shooting on my birthday in the middle of May. It never classed as sport because the quarry were young rooks, just ready to leave the nest. They perched, swaying on the topmost twigs of stately elms, to be picked off by the men with rifles down below. It was no birthday treat for me or, I suspect, any of the other folk who went. It was regarded purely as an exercise in controlling vermin, precisely as ferreting for rats was. Those who didn't turn up to do their stint would not be invited to go rabbiting later in the season.

I never quite understood why farmers had rooks on their blacklist. The only reason they ever gave me was that rooks would march along their rows of corn, when it had just nicely sprouted, and pull it out by the roots. This was perfectly true. I have watched rooks uprooting corn myself. But the grain had, by then, been transformed into root and they were not interested in eating the morsels of grain that had survived. The attraction for them were the wireworms that had already attacked the crop long before the rooks arrived. The rooks were really doing the farmers a good turn by eating the insect pests that attacked their crops, so I always had a conscience about shooting them and spent more time talking to my fellow guests than getting down to business.

Times have altered since those pre-war days and rooks have more to worry about than a few chaps with guns knocking off their fledglings. Dutch elm disease has decimated the old traditional rookeries, where generation after generation of the birds congregated to breed. They seem to prefer elms to nest in over any other tree, although we had a small rookery in lime trees by our back door at the last house we lived in. But it was astonishing to see how loyal they were to the trees where their ancestors had bred for years before.

135

I use the M5 to the West Country pretty often, where I was amazed to see that rooks persisted in nesting in elms long after the disease had killed them. It blew holes through the country superstition that if rooks forsake their rookery it is a sign that the trees, if not the owner as well, are about to die. At the other extreme I noticed a rookery in young trees by the M1 the other day that were so low you could have knocked them off with a tennis racquet, never mind a .22 rifle.

In any case, there are far fewer rooks than there were in my young days. The main cause is chemical pesticides, which farmers spew on their land to combat insects. They kill the insects and the birds that eat them and it is high time our scientists got down to concocting poisons that are more selective and less persistent.

Snowy

Just after the war a rat-catcher from Sussex phoned to ask if I wanted a young albino rook that had fallen out of the nest. Rooks are normally so black that their plumage shines with a sort of iridescent blue bloom that is really blacker than black. For such densely coloured birds to throw a white freak seemed very strange indeed. So I reared the young bird and installed him in a large aviary where he could fly freely, and, without much originality, called him Snowy!

I took a few photographs of him and wrote a few articles in magazines read by naturalists I thought would be interested, without getting much response. Then, the following May, I got a cryptic postcard from a strange vicar buried in the wilds of Sussex. 'Sir, I understand that the albino rook, poached from my rookery, fell into your hands. There is another this year. Do you want it?' it said. Even I was somewhat abashed. I wrote apologetically, saying my rat-catcher friend had omitted to mention he'd nicked it, but it was marvellously tame – and I was sure it would like a companion!

So I motored to Sussex, made my peace with the vicar, who had a great sense of humour, and brought Frosty back, to live with Snowy. They were delightfully tame and intelligent and became great favourites with the family.

If any rooks have diseased trees in their rookery, they are more than welcome to build their rookery in our wood! We have neither elms nor rook shooters.

52. Haymaking

When I was a kid, haymaking was a great excitement at this time of year. The fields were cut with mowing machines that had wicked, triangular knives that oscillated over fixed 'fingers', nipping the long grass off at ground level, and leaving it in neat swaths running the length of the field. Keeping the knives sharp was a skilled job, for each triangular section had to be honed to razor-edge with a fairly smooth file. There were no clever jigs by which to gauge the angles; no grinding wheels to take the irk out of the work. Success depended solely on the craftsmanship of the chap who got his machine in fettle.

Stones in the grass, fallen boughs from storm-struck trees or any other hazard could ruin the whole operation, so that the mown field looked as if it had been gnawed into ragged tussocks instead of barbered clean. The mowing machine was pulled by two carthorses, or three if the crop was exceptionally heavy or the blade was long enough to cut a swath more than about four feet wide.

That was when I came into my own, because it was useful to have a kid to take the lead horse by the bridle to make sure the machine kept to the precise line on corners at the end of the field. Better still, I was sometimes allowed to ride on the lead horse's back, guiding him at corners, but free to look down on the world until crisis broke.

When the grass was cut it was left to ripen in the swaths where it had fallen for a day or so, depending on the weather. Good haymaking weather was sunny, with enough wind to drive the moisture from the fallen crop, so, when the top was dried, the whole crop was turned over to dry the underside. It was turned manually, using large wooden rakes with wooden teeth three or four inches long. The head of the rake was about two foot six, so that an energetic worker could work down the swath at almost walking pace.

I tried to be 'there gone' – or missing – when the time came to turn

Building ricks was a labour-intensive job, made obsolete by machines. (See the photograph on page 81 for a contrast with today's highly rationalised farming techniques)

the hay. It was not only very hard work, but also very boring. Mothers, wives and sisters were press-ganged into such dull routine, but I tried to get fixed-up on the horse rake whenever possible. This contraption had long, curved tines, which scooped up the swaths and deposited them in large heaps, ready to be loaded on to hay wains, with pitchforks, before carting to the stack yard to be built into ricks. The whole laborious process was slug slow and ruinously expensive in labour costs, by modern standards – but great fun to look back on.

Such good old days have gone. Very few people even bother to make hay now, although the drudgery has been mechanised. The modern fashion is silage. The grass is cut, as it used to be for hay, but, instead of drying it carefully, until it is 'made', it is only allowed to wilt. When it droops like flowers condemned by flower arrangers, it is collected into clamps or pits, where it is compressed and ferments into a fragrant pudding, if it's right.

Unfortunately, silage is not always 'right', and sour silage has a pong worse than mating ferrets.

Now we are getting rain, after the long dry spell, the grass will grow so fast that you'll have to jump clear to avoid being engulfed. Many farmers will be making silage and clamping it before it has wilted, to cash-in on the bounty. Then we are in for trouble that never afflicted haymakers. The liquor that drains from silage clamps is both poisonous and prone to go rotten. If it gets into brooks and ditches, it can be far more poisonous than the run-off from chemical pesticides because it is so much more highly concentrated. A four-hundred ton clamp of unwilted silage can produce as much pollution as the untreated sewage from a town the size of Shrewsbury. It is four times as strong as piggery slurry and 150 times as strong as crude human sewage.

Such 'advances' in agricultural science cut costs because they save labour and, when they are done right, there is much to be said for them. But, like stubble burning and chemical pesticides, they can also create pollution in the countryside as bad as any factory in towns.

Rose-tinted specs are not necessary to make old-fashioned hay-making seem more attractive.

53. *The Eagle Has Landed in a Legal Row**

The Wildlife and Countryside Act is a dog's breakfast of a bill which tries to please everyone and succeeds in making fools of its sponsors almost every time it is challenged.

There have been ructions in the Highlands this June because a Scottish laird is quoted as condoning applications for a government permit to shoot a golden eagle. Golden eagles are not inconspicuous birds, having a wingspan of six feet when adult, and it takes a lot of food to keep them satisfied. They prey on the blue mountain hares, which thrive in the heather-clad Highlands. They will make do with smaller game, ranging from rats and mice and rabbits to weakly calves of red deer. And, in common with most predatory hawks and falcons, golden eagles are lazy and not too choosy. They are not above eating carrion and making a meal from dead animals – saves the trouble of catching them.

This nearly led to their downfall because there are hundreds of dead lambs in the hills every spring, which are welcomed as feasts by foxes and eagles, buzzards and wild cats.

Hill farmers are commonly regarded as hit-and-miss 'dog-and-stick' chaps who leave more than they should to chance. They turn their sheep out on the hills and leave them to lamb as best they can. Weather is often atrocious at lambing time and food is scarce, so that it is considered quite good, in the Highlands, for ewes to average one lamb apiece while properly shepherded lowland flocks will average almost twice the number. The reason, quite simply, is that dog-and-stick farmers find it cheaper to allow for a high casualty rate among their flocks than to spend a lot of money in extra food and labour to rear a higher percentage.

During the drought this spring, many lambs in the Highlands have been abnormally weak because the ewes have been short of milk, and

*This article was originally published in June 1984.

Aerobatics beyond compare. Golden eagle in full flight

the average ratio has frequently fallen below a lamb per ewe. Lambs which die are left to rot – or for Nature's scavengers to clean up – so that predators have had some very easy pickings. Crofters recently saw a golden eagle feeding on the carcase of a lamb and, returning later, saw an eagle swoop on a lamb and lift it, struggling, into the air. It was a bit too much for it, and the lamb escaped, but the crofters jumped to the conclusion that all the ewes which had no lambs must have been robbed by the eagle.

They were visited by a member of the Nature Conservancy Council and the representative of the Royal Society for the Protection of Birds, and the conclusion they reached was that there was no doubt that eagles will eat dead lambs but that the only living ones attacked were probably so weak already that they would have died in any case.

However, Lord Burton of Dochfour, chairman of the local fox club, took the matter up and suggested applying for a licence, under the Wildlife and Countryside Act, to kill the eagle as a pest. A member of the Bass brewing family, he is scarcely likely to be short of the price of a pint, so the assumption is that it is not so much the loss of a few lambs that inspired him as the opportunity to test the strength of the Wildlife and Countryside Act.

Conservationists, on the other hand, realise that golden eagles are not only rare but in grave danger of extinction if licences are granted to shoot them on suspicion of taking weakly lambs, which would only have added to the mutton mountain if they had survived.

One of the major weaknesses in the Wildlife and Countryside Act is that it makes a lot of pious promises to conserve wildlife and lays down penalties for killing all sorts of threatened creatures, from barn owls and kingfishers to herons, unless it can be shown that they are doing damage to property or crops. A heron catching fish or an eagle finishing off a weakly lamb could be construed as doing damage, but to issue a licence for execution on such grounds would simply make an ass of the law.

Fortunately there are dim chinks of light to indicate that the law is tightening up. Last Monday, two Coventry men were fined £200 each and their car and equipment confiscated at Dornoch Sheriff's court, for taking the eggs of protected birds. I trust the Sheriff will be as tough with people who kill eagles and that the Secretary of State for Scotland will refuse a licence to kill them legally.

54. My Ferret Could Teach Farmers Some Tricks

Farmers at the Royal Show this week have been boasting about the high 'food conversion rates' they have achieved with their stock. It is obvious that a chap who can produce a pound of beef or pork by feeding less food than his competitors is going to make more profit. They have discovered that quite a lot of food is used up not in growing heavier, but simply to keep warm. So, by keeping their animal houses at the right temperature, they can grow cheaper meat than competitors who don't bother about such trifles.

They were all going on about their big motor cars and other signs of success and I couldn't help smiling because I reckon that my old jill ferret could teach most of them how to go on. She really is a marvel. She had a litter in the last week in May, though I couldn't tell how many because ferrets (like many other animals which can be tamed but are not truly 'domesticated') are very subject to stress when they have just had their young. Poking into the nest and disturbing them, and, worst of all, tainting the young with the smell of humans, will sometimes distress the mother so much that she will eat them!

I knew she had 'kitted' because I could hear the faint squeaks and whimpers coming from her nest as the youngsters learned to suckle her. I didn't look at them for about a week but I could tell from the size of the old jill's udder that she had got a litter that was really taxing her capacity to satisfy them with milk. The normal size of ferrets' litters is about five or six, though I once had a jill that produced ten. My ferret this year has topped the lot because, when she was thoroughly accustomed to being a mum, I gently poked the nest apart and could hardly believe my eyes when I counted a litter of twelve!

144

The author introduces a ferret to Tick

No farmer can be good at his job unless he is also a competent naturalist – and most naturalists are natural stockmen. So much depends on giving animals conditions as similar to their life in the wild as possible. I know from experience that stoats, which are closely related to ferrets, move their litters to several nests while they are rearing them. Close confinement, in a small nest, provides just the conditions for parasites, like fleas, to breed. So the mother takes them to a fresh nest before insects have time to breed.

I do not keep ferrets in a little hutch because they are such active creatures that it fills my eyes with pleasure to watch them gambolling in sinuous play in as large a run as possible. They take so much spectacular exercise that they are in perfect trim when I want to send them down a hole or into a woodpile to make rats hiding there bolt out for the dogs. My ferrets live in an old brick outhouse which was once used as a dog kennel, with a large wire netting run outside. Inside the outhouse are two wooden boxes, with entrance holes cut in the sides so that the ferret can creep into her ready-made straw-filled nest. When one nest gets a bit stale, she carries the lot to the other by the scruff of their necks, and I replace the bedding she has spurned.

I have been absolutely astonished at how fast those ferret kittens have grown. They are now about five weeks old, though they look younger because ferrets are blind for so long that their eyes are only just beginning to open. When they were born, they were about as big as mice. I weighed them yesterday and they averaged half a pound apiece! I weighed the mother too, and she was exactly a pound and three quarters. So, if my arithmetic is right, an animal has produced a litter almost four times her own weight in under five weeks! To do so, she has had to eat the food and convert it into milk because the young ferrets don't scramble out of the nest until their eyes are beginning to open.

If farmers at the Royal Show could produce a cow that could produce four times her own weight in beef or a sheep that could produce four times her weight in lambs, they could give away their Mercedes and all swan around in Rolls-Royces!

As well as feeding her litter so well, the old jill has kept them as neatly groomed as fashion models and their faint musky odour is as seductive as expensive after-shave lotion!

Soon, when their eyes are properly open, they will feed themselves and play around as actively and prettily as leaves in the vortex of an autumn wind!

55. Biological Pest Control

A favourite quarry in the modern blood sport of farmer-bashing is the chap who kills his weeds with chemical sprays. If one manufacturer invents a concoction to kill greenfly in twenty minutes, his competitor sets out to find one that will do the job in a few minutes less. I would respect him more if he set out to produce a substance that was safer and more selective and less persistent.

So the pressure I would like to see applied would be to license dangerous chemicals only for a limited period, say five years. After that time it would be a criminal offence to manufacture, sell or use them. This would force manufacturers to commission research into safer rather than quicker methods of crop protection.

So many of these chemicals do not restrict their venom to the particular pest that is troubling the farmer. Some of them are lethal to anything from a bull to a bullfinch that happens to get a dose by mistake. Not unnaturally, organisations such as the Royal Society for the Protection of Birds get stroppy when their members discover that such innocent rarities as Red Kites, and common species like the thrushes in our garden, all suffer the fate that was designed – by the boffins – for creatures that cut into farmers' profits.

Even the scientists are growing so concerned about public criticism that they are starting to bark up another tree. 'Biological control' is the in-phrase for being really selective about the victims under sentence of death. The example that almost everybody knows is the case of ladybirds and greenfly. Ladybirds lay eggs which hatch out into the little black insects that look like a cross between a woodlouse and a beetle. These ladybird larvae love nothing so well as greenfly for their supper, and Nature is often wise enough to send a countless army of ladybirds in years when greenfly are a plague. If scientists can organise conditions that are ideal for ladybirds to breed in when

147

This blue tit has built its nest in a chest of drawers in a barn

greenfly are a plague, there will be no need for the poisons that are sprayed at present which kill friend and foe indiscriminately.

Controlling pests by encouraging creatures that prey on them or diseases that kill the pests but don't damage other creatures is the new science of biological control. The Forestry Commission, which is far more advanced than the Ministry of Agriculture, tried it some years ago on Cannock Chase. That season there was a plague of pine looper moths. They wreak havoc on pine trees. It so happens that looper caterpillars are a favourite diet of blue tits, so a camera was set up to film the tit every time she visited the nest to feed her young. The focus was so sharp that it was possible to count how many caterpillars she took at each visit. By multiplying this by the number of visits, it was possible to calculate how many caterpillars the tits accounted for each day.

The next step was to erect nest boxes further into the trees than tits normally went. In this way, enough birds would take up residence to conquer the plague of loopers.

That was an early example of biological control, which did no accidental damage to anything but 'target' species! I have just tried an experiment in biological control of my own. Three years ago we felled the pine trees on a few acres of wood and spent the money they fetched on replanting with Christmas trees, to be harvested a few years from now. The snag was that, when the old pines were cleared, a positive jungle of young birch, bramble, mountain ash, and every species we didn't want, shot up to smother the young trees we did want. It cost a fortune to weed them out! The next year we cleared a patch and left it unfenced for a season. All the 'weed' species came as before, but this time they have not flourished – because the deer ate every one. We then fenced the desert they left and planted our young Christmas trees which have flourished because the deer had done the weeding before the next crop was planted. An example of biological control which has satisfied all and damaged none!

56. *Sad Lament at the Barber Shop*

When I was a kid, sixty years ago, there was a barber down the seedy end of Stafford Street in Walsall, who had other profitable sidelines. I think his name was Hitch, but the shop was widely known as 'Itch's', which was more appropriate than the customers probably realised because the barber made more money from selling cage birds than he did from cutting hair. The whole shop reeked of warm feathers and fusty bird seed and cages which were only cleaned out when business was slack.

Mr Itch's scissors snipped to a constant background of birds, fluttering against the bars in futile efforts to escape, because his merchandise was not broods of sleek budgerigars or sweet singing canaries, bred for a life of captivity. This barber's birds had all been caught in nets or traps or on sticky bird-lime plastered on to thistle heads. When small birds descended to feed there, the bird-lime stuck to their feathers and prevented them flying away.

There were goldfinches, sold as seven-coloured linnets, and skylarks and starlings, with tongues slit to make them talk. Although it was commonplace then, I am glad to say it would be illegal now, outlawed by various Protection of Birds Acts passed in the last half-century.

I hated to see them, but I didn't visit Mr Itch to buy a bird, nor even to have my hair cut. I visited him in my summer holidays to buy a muslin net on a bamboo cane which he sold for the modest price of thru'pence, the equivalent of just over a penny in our modern worthless washers which masquerade as money. It was a week's pocket money to me and I could only afford it in the first few days of my holidays, after which I was spent up. But I knew from experience that I would get hours and hours more pleasure by investing in a net than I would have done from the equivalent in gobstoppers or liquorice allsorts.

My dog and I wandered off on our own, with Mr Itch's net and one of my mother's jam jars, to try our luck in the many 'swags' or pools left by mining subsidence that pockmarked the countryside in those days. They were weedy pools. Some of them were also deep and dangerous but they were sniving (or teeming) with newts and water beetles and Jack Bannocks – their proper name was sticklebacks and they had a row of spines running along their backs, which could be raised in threat or anger. They could also be raised involuntarily, for when they died and stiffened in pallid rigor mortis they floated, belly uppermost, with spines raised in protest against the unnatural captivity in the jam jars we took to carry them home.

In retrospect, I realise that I was probably as cruel to put the graceful little fish in such a tiny prison as Mr Itch was to sell larks in cages no larger than a hand could span. But it never struck either of us at the time, not because we were cruel and callous but simply because we couldn't have mustered a spark of imagination between us.

Mr Itch has long gone where the only wings are on angels and his barber's shop has been ground into the earth by slum-clearing bulldozers, so I didn't buy a net from there when I wanted one recently. I had to make my own. But a bit of nylon netting, disciplined into shape by stiff wire, bent into a circle and fixed to a stick with an old jubilee clip, made a better net for no more money. I spent hours poking about among the pond weed in a friend's pool, making blind dates with the fish which took wrong turnings into my questing net. This time my captives were lucky because they were never imprisoned in jam jars. I popped a score or so into a large bucket of water which was quickly slipped into our pool across the paddock. It was rather a sterile pool when we came because it fills from the wood which is carpeted with acid peat. It has taken years to find water plants which can grow in such acid water. But I found a pool in the wood across our boundary which has water of similar type and water plants which seem to thrive there.

Last year, we dredged a tractor trailer-full of this weed and transplanted it to our pool, where it is thriving in luxury. It should make the perfect habitat for the shoal of Jack Bannocks which I have enjoyed catching on a fishing expedition which rekindled some of my happiest memories.

57. *Wildlife is Priority in the Big Shake-up**

The Forestry Commission has just announced a reorganisation which may have profound effects on wildlife, especially in the Midlands. In the last twenty years the Commission labour force has slumped by more than half, from 10,973 to 4,749. Few will quarrel with the intention to have a hearty shakeout, but it is vital to ensure that wildlife does not suffer in the process.

During the two World Wars every available tree was converted to timber, so the Forestry Commission was instructed to replace the loss. An oak tree which takes two minutes to fell will take as many centuries to replace. Even a common pine will take a generation. So early foresters planted millions of trees in regimented rows to minimise the labour of weeding them.

Environmentalists were up in arms when miles of glorious mountain scenery was blotted out by miserable grey foreign pines. They were furious that similar, unimaginative barrack squares of conifers turned 'natural' lowland landscapes into bureaucratic draughtboards.

The modern sport of farmer-bashing was, as yet, unknown, so foresters were the butts of public scorn. The early foresters also asked for all they got. They trapped badgers for making runs under netting which let rabbits into young plantations; they shot red squirrels for eating seed; and they drove deer to men waiting with shotguns, which killed some and let others creep away to die a slow and agonising death. Public disgust was so fierce that the Forestry Commission engaged Herbert Fooks, who had a distinguished reputation as conservationist, to polish up its image. He decided to reverse much of the then current practice. He made badger gates, which excluded rabbits but allowed badgers into plantations, where they do nothing but good by eating voles, beetles and other pests of trees. He wanted deer selectively controlled by rifles to allow as many to survive as the

152

* This article was originally published in August 1984.

terrain could support without unacceptable damage. He decided to encourage as much wildlife as possible instead of as little.

Old-fashioned foresters reckoned that their mission was to grow trees at any price. They did not care what was sacrificed in the process, so Herbert Fooks found that he was banging his head against a very obstructive wall. The shining exception was Jack Chard, the conservator at Chester, who was responsible for forests from the Lake District, down the Welsh border and over to Warwickshire. His patch included the Dukeries and Cannock Chase. I have known and re-spected him since we were founder members of the Mammal Society, many years ago, so I was delighted when he chose, as his first trainee,

Cannock Chase

Gerald Springthorpe, another old friend, who was then warrener at Cannock Chase.

Between them, they forged a revolutionary policy for wildlife which has become a model for the rest of the country. Deer herds have grown in number and improved in quality; badgers have reappeared where they were absent for decades; and there is still a colony of wild red squirrels at Cannock although they have been replaced by grey in most parts of the country.

Good money is no longer thrown after bad in futile efforts to make trees grow in wet patches and other unsuitable habitats. They are reserved instead for reptiles or wetland-loving birds. Areas are set aside for butterflies, orchids, nightjars or other rarities which would have been extinguished under the old regime, for no significant rise in production.

A yardstick of the success of the Forestry Commission's new policy for wildlife is that the Royal Society for the Protection of Birds – which used to be among forestry's bitchiest critics – now does joint research at Cannock, with Gerald Springthorpe and his men. The Nature Conservancy Council is helping him by encouraging colonies of bats to nest in bat boxes made by Commission personnel.

There is also an educational museum second to none at Cannock. The policy is to start 'em young, and Forest Rangers are helped by a guide that would do credit to higher education.

The result has been of incalculable benefit to wildlife, and the progressive policy has done more to restore public confidence in the Commission than an army of public relations consultants. The tiny minority of bureaucratic deadbeats must not be allowed to reverse the process in the guise of reorganisation.

58. *Nothing Glorious – About Sunday*

Grouse shooting won't start on the 'Glorious Twelfth' this year, for the simple reason is that 12th August falls on Sunday – and it is illegal to shoot game on the Sabbath. The season will therefore begin on the 13th, and in some parts, Monday 13th promises to be an unlucky day for grouse shooters. This is because some animal welfare groups have threatened to organise mass trespasses on to grouse moors, to disturb the grouse before the sportsmen arrive and to get in the way when they do.

The rights and wrongs of shooting grouse aside, it is worth speculating on what effect on the countryside a law prohibiting it might have. Environmentalists often protest about any change to the countryside, from grubbing out hedgerows or filling in small pools, to covering our hills with foreign softwood trees. The reason that wild moorland is so attractive is that mile upon mile of rolling purple heather gives a marvellous sense of space and solitude that is a mental tonic after a week cooped up in city offices or factories. The heather-clad moorland, where grouse shatter the silence with repetitive cries of 'Go-bak, Go-bak' (presumably to mass trespassers as well as grouse shooters!), gives the impression of timelessness.

But not all moorlands are what they seem. A couple of thousand years ago, the countryside was so well clothed by woodland that it is said a red squirrel could pass from tree to tree, from Land's End to John O'Groats, without ever touching the ground. What we see as moorlands today were then forests of scrub oak and other natural hardwood trees. But as time went on the trees were felled – and often burned – to make clearings for primitive agriculture. Clearings which were not tilled were grazed by sheep and cattle which ate seedling trees as greedily as grass.

As industry began to flourish, whole forests were cut down and

Shooting driven grouse from a wooden slatted 'butt' on the threatened moor-lands

areas like Cannock Chase were stripped to make charcoal for smelting steel or making glass. Nobody bothered about restoring 'waste' land in those days, so heather colonised large areas that had previously been blanketed by woodland.

Heatherclad moorlands are now under even greater threat. The stupid Common Market policy of paying subsidies for sheep to make mountains of surplus mutton (which has to be sold at a loss) results in overgrazing moors with sheep. Sheep like heather but, if there are too many of them, they eat all the young shoots before they can develop, eventually killing it off. They are also infested with sheep ticks, which irritate them but carry fatal disease for grouse. So overgrazing by sheep kills heather which is replaced by bracken or coarse grass which sheep will not eat, making the moorland valueless for them. They also diminish the grouse stock which lowers the sporting rent. In the past moors that are not too heavily stocked with sheep have produced enough rent to pay gamekeepers to 'manage' the moor for grouse.

Left to itself, heather grows lanky and stringy, good neither as food nor nesting cover. So the keeper divides up the moors into blocks, which he burns by rotation, over a number of years, always setting fire to the long, sterile, stringy stuff. Next season it will sprout out as tender shoots which are the vital food of young grouse chicks, and the fringe benefit is that sheep like it too. The result of this skilled keeping is that well-managed moors are a glorious patchwork of healthy heather, at different stages of growth, giving wide variety of scenery.

Without such management, vast areas of moorland would revert to bracken or scrub grass. This would be uneconomic for either grouse or sheep. The alternative would be for those who want access there to pay for its management, the equivalent of sporting rents (which are very high), or to convert it to softwood forests which would destroy the view and be as useless for leisure as they would be for sheep or grouse.

59. A Precious Commodity

Threats of water rationing in Devon and elsewhere, if the summer drought persists, have prompted suggestions of a 'water grid', similar in principle to the national grid, which feeds electricity from scattered power stations to wherever it is needed. The difference would be that high-voltage electricity is fed through cables, stitched by pylons across the face of the countryside, while water would be fed through underground pipes. The cost would be astronomic.

It is easy enough to blame the present shortage on the drought because, if not the worst in living memory, it is certainly the worst since 1976, with its recent memories of standpipes and water carts. But the drought is not the only cause.

Our house is a mile from the mains supply on the main road and we were very short last year, when there wasn't a drought. The trouble was eventually traced to the fact that the number of cows being milked in the area had increased four or five times and the new regulations on hygiene caused far more water to be used for washing down. The total consumption in our very rural area had more than doubled so that demand had outstripped the ability of the company pumps to supply what was being used.

When my wife bought a new clothes-washing machine, I asked the makers how much water it used because we pay for our water by the meter. I was told that it used seven gallons a cycle. I was *not told* that there were several cycles to each wash! When I checked for myself, I discovered that a load of washing used more than twenty gallons. I had shut the stable door after the horse had gone because I had by then paid for the machine.

But it drove home to me the fact that water is not just something that comes out of the tap. It is a precious commodity, to be valued like pure air or beautiful landscape. We squander it at our peril.

A prime selling point of cars is the number of miles they do to the gallon. I should like it to be stated that equipment using water performed the function it was sold for on fewer gallons of water than its rivals used, to give makers the incentive to sell thrifty machines.

But it is useless to persuade consumers to be economical when Big Brother, in Whitehall, pays subsidies for waste. The suicidal craze for growing more and more food, at *any* price, has seduced the Ministry of Agriculture to fork out about £20 million a year for land drainage projects. They lower the level of rivers so that farmers can put in land drains to convert water meadows into more profitable prairies of corn.

When it rained the water used to soak into the land, which conserved the water as efficiently as a sponge. The rivers are now converted into glorified drains, which sluice the water down to the sea, instead of conserving it and releasing it gradually.

'Cumecs' is the with-it boffins' jargon for measuring success and cumecs are the number of cubic metres per second of water raging downstream. These cumecs not only waste water but destroy riverside wildlife in the process. The Nature Conservancy Council, normally a lethargic bunch, are so incensed by the effect on wildlife that they have been stung into issuing an expensive brochure, *Nature Conservation and River Engineering*, which gives graphic illustrations of lazy, tree-fringed rivers, rich in wildlife, which have been turned into drains as unattractive as city sewers. At the risk of teaching their grandmothers to suck eggs, they have told the water authorities how to improve the flow in rivers without ruining them for wildlife and amenity.

More damage has been done to some of the most beautiful of our rivers by insensitive drainage authorities than could be done by an army of mechanised vandals, so let's applaud the Nature Conservancy Council for trying. But I still wonder if they are not putting the cart before the horse.

It seems a crime to me to sacrifice our precious wetlands on the altar of drainage to the sea when the real priorities are surely to economise by treating water as the priceless resource it is and to use our wetlands and river meadows to conserve water, as Nature intended, instead of allowing 'clever' engineers to sluice our assets down the drain.

60. His Master's Dog

A recent gift of a punnet of luscious ripe mulberries revived old memories of my schooldays. It was an odd association of thought because stewed mulberries is one of my favourite dishes – and, whatever the pundits say, my schooldays were anything but the happiest days of my life. But the mulberries reminded me of a great, spreading tree near to the place where I slept. The trunk was gnarled and thick; the branches rivalled the proverbial spreading chestnut, under which the blacksmith sat, and the lowest branch was about six feet from the ground.

The headmaster had a dog called Thorn. He was a great brute of a dog, a cross between an Airedale and a collie, rough-coated with a deep-throated bark that made the Hound of the Baskervilles sound as effete as an alto choirboy. I remember the bark particularly because, as dusk was falling on summer evenings, Thorn went to the mulberry tree and leaped at the lower branch, scarring it with his fangs and bellowing out his hatred. As there was nobody around and nothing unusual up the tree, it was puzzling to decide what was making him so furious and the popular theory was that he had once chased a cat up the tree and never forgiven it for not coming down to be killed! My own feeling was that Thorn was far too frenzied to have been turned on by a memory. My somewhat vivid imagination conjured up visions of the old dog worrying some wretched cat, whose ghost sat safely aloft and taunted him for the rest of his life.

My punnet of mulberries triggered a whole saga of memories of the old dog – some of which were more vivid than others. The youngest kids were given menial tasks that fitted them, in later life, for being dogsbodies, if not moguls of industry. It was a form of discipline against which I soon rebelled but, while it lasted, one of my tasks was to find Thorn, wherever he had settled, and take him to the head-

160

master's study, where he slept away the night in state, while I dossed down in an uncomfortable school bed.

I had always been closely involved with dogs and was well used to having dogs which did what they were told. However allergic to discipline I may have been myself, I expected instant obedience from my dogs. I have never put up with fools, either human or canine, gladly, and 'Do as I say, if not as I do' has always been my motto. So that first night I wandered round aimlessly till I spotted Thorn asleep in the middle of the lawn. The lawn was out of bounds to boys, so I called out: 'Thorn, good dog. Come on.' Thorn took not the slightest notice and it was clear, from the sarcasm of the other kids, that they did not think I was as good with dogs as I had made out.

Rules or no rules, I marched boldly onto the lawn, caught the rebel hound by the collar, and started to walk off with him. If the old dog had taken the slightest notice of commands from boys, his life would obviously have been a misery, so he stuck his ground. Unaccustomed to such defiance, I tugged unceremoniously at his collar. He was not used to such insolence, so he caught my forearm in a grip of iron. The scar remains, to hammer home the mulberry memories, so when he let go, I made my exit.

I had no intention of being beaten, so went down to the kitchen and nicked a hunk of meat and took it back as a peace offering. The old dog fell for the ruse and followed me back to the privacy of my study, where I made a muzzle from a bootlace, and gave him the father and mother of good hidings.

It did my stock good with the headmaster, who never suspected such treachery, and marvelled at how quickly I had 'won his dog's confidence and inspired his devotion'! It did me good in other ways. A lad in my study, whose only claim to fame was that his father was a bishop, was a terrible bully and made my life hell. So I held Thorn by the collar, and trod gently on his toe. The old dog had no intention of calling my bluff twice, but growled as if he would eat me. Commanding him to attack my oppressor, I pretended to be holding him back by the collar. The bishop's bullying son was not sharp enough to realise that Thorn was growling not at him, but me. He bribed me with bull's-eyes to keep the dog at bay and transferred his oppression to other kids who couldn't handle dogs.

61. Robin's Forest

I spent a marvellous day among the ancient oaks of Sherwood Forest last week. It was genuine primaeval forest, exactly the same now as it must have always been. That isn't to say that nothing has changed, because the countryside cannot be 'frozen' and preserved, like trout in aspic, as woolly environmentalists would so often like to do. They complain about fields getting larger and woods getting smaller, about old trees being felled and others, sometimes softwoods they do not like, being planted in their stead.

But the countryside has always been changing – and it will continue to change – except in a very few places like the part of Sherwood Forest I discovered last week. And, like the countryman who finds a crop of mushrooms, nothing would induce me to share the secret of exactly where it is because crowds following in my wake would disturb the wildlife there!

I wandered into a clearing among enormous oak trees, mostly fairly stubby and apparently stunted because they seemed almost as far round the girth as they were high. This was because the custom in olden days was to 'pollard' oak trees as the willows along lazy river banks are pollarded. The branches were lopped off, eight or ten feet from the ground, and the wood was used for fuel, often for smelting iron or making glass. The stumps of the cut branches sprouted shoots, which deer or cattle would have loved – if the lowest available had not been left out of reach deliberately by the woodmen. These branches grew far more quickly than seedlings would have grown, even if they had escaped damage by rabbits or hares or deer or sheep, because they had the whole root system of a mature tree to feed them.

One great tree, under whose shade I sat to eat my sandwiches, was probably a venerable veteran when Robin Hood was chasing Maid Marian around the bushes. Some trees, even older, had run their

An ancient pollarded oak in Sherwood Forest

span, died in dignity and quietly subsided back to the earth from which an acorn had sprouted long centuries ago.

Tidy-minded little bureaucrats, who lay out city parks, would have flipped their tiny minds and cleared the rotting timber out of the way – but there was nobody to mess about with gaudy flower beds in that wild spot.

Every now and then, the silence was split by the cries of wood-peckers and, while I was sitting quietly munching my sandwiches, a dappled deer and her fawn came out to graze in a clearing fifty yards away. It hammered home the point that men with the woodcraft of Robin Hood and Little John would have had no difficulty in knocking-off the King's game with their bows and arrows!

To our generation, which visualises forests as endless row after row of planted trees, genuine 'wild' forest, like Sherwood, emphasises not only how much the cultivated countryside has changed, but how much even the meaning of the terms we use has changed. The map said that, close by where I sat, was a 'forest lawn', but it did not mean the weedless patch we think of, shorn bare by mechanical devices. Ancient forest lawns were clearings hewn from the forest to allow grasses and herbs to flourish naturally to feed the deer and cattle.

On the edge of my clearing was one solitary oak, apparently growing through the centre of a rock of solid stone, about ten feet in diameter. What had really happened was than an acorn, centuries ago, had sprouted in soil that covered the rock. The roots couldn't go down, so they had crept over the surface of the rock till they found soil at the edge – and then they had gone down for water and nourishment. Over the years, the roots had grown thicker than a man's arm till they imprisoned the rock like a jewel in its clasp. There it had been for generations and there it will be for generations yet to come. It made me feel quite young!

62. Old Dogs and New Tricks

Tough, my first Alsatian, was the perfect yard dog. I do not mean by that, that she lived in the yard. She always slept in my study, which has a door opening out on to the yard and paddock where the laying hens live. This meant she could sleep in the comfort of my room but had the run of about half an acre outside the back door, which was fenced-in, to keep her from straying and to stop intruders from getting right up to the house.

Tough was very alert and rushed from the study like a roaring tornado at the least strange sound outside. She was also very sweet-tempered and her bark was far worse than her bite. This enabled me to teach her several parlour tricks. One was that, if I hissed quietly under my breath, she rushed off, roaring defiance more in the hope of finding someone to bark at than in any expectation of making a capture. If anyone strange had been in the wood, she put her nose to the ground and cast around like a fox hound. A quiet hiss from me gave her the go-ahead to search, and she would follow the scent till she found the intruder, and then bark round him till I arrived. She didn't bite him, just prevented him moving, but it seemed to have a demoralising effect and I never remember the same trespasser returning to be winkled out a second time.

When Tough died, I tried to get another pup from the police, where she had come from, but they told me that so many of the Alsatians they acquired developed hip dysplasia, a hereditary defect that gets progressively worse. So I didn't risk it but bought Tick, my German short-haired pointer, instead. But when she died, I did get another Alsatian, Belle, to run with her.

Belle is a nice bitch but she isn't as sweet-natured as Tough was and I daren't risk sending her to hold someone up till I arrive to investigate. When the sound of her barking stopped, I fear that it would be because her mouth was full of intruder. But, as happens with far too many dogs bred for show, cosmetic good looks in her family have taken priority over good health. She is showing signs of the dreaded hip dysplasia and I fear that her days are numbered.

We got Tarka, a German Rottweiler pup, a couple of years ago as a companion for Belle, and she has been a great success. Rottweilers are used by the German police because they are 'harder' and more determined than Alsatians and German police are not so fussy as ours if a criminal gets pinned. With the spate of thugs robbing houses and mugging their inmates, a dog which will hold an intruder till the police arrive is a great comfort in isolated houses like ours, and I would rather steal a bone from a safari-park lion than come into our house uninvited.

But Tarka is rather trade-union minded. She is allergic to overtime and unsocial hours and she is not quite as alert as an Alsatian. It is always Belle who gets the first whiff of an alarm – and Tarka who joins in the fun. So I am looking out for a new Alsatian pup to follow old Belle and to act as the prompter to alert Tarka when there is anyone strange about. I shan't make the mistake of getting a beautiful, low-slung bitch like Belle again, because so many of the show types are unsound. I shall look, instead, for a tall, rangy, wolfish-bred pup which would never get far in the show ring. Her mother must be a bold, alert dog who will obviously stand no nonsense from anyone, and the pup must be no more than seven weeks old when I collect her.

63. *Where the Grass is Greener*

Having just come home from a week filming the September TV sheep dog trials on the Chatsworth Estate in Derbyshire, it has dawned on me just how much difference a few miles and vertical feet can make to weather.

We have had the drought of all time and our three pools are lower than they have ever been since we came to Goat Lodge, twenty-odd years ago. The pool by the house is filled from a ditch that collects surface water in our wood and from the old deer park, which has been reclaimed for arable fields by the neighbouring farmer. 'Reclaimed' is not an accurate description, because it had never been cultivated before. It was originally part of the ancient Forest of Needwood and clearings had simply been made, to leave a deer park and odd patches of woodland. It was impossible to plough it because there were too many roots of ancient oaks that had been struck by lightning or felled in days gone by.

When we came, our ditch started, at the end of the wood, from the overflow of a horse trough, marked 'spring' on the Ordnance map and, whatever the weather, there was always a trickle of water to keep the level of the pool more or less constant.

When my neighbour reclaimed the park, he really cultivated it for the first time. The whole surface was varicose-veined with drains, which sluiced rainfall directly into major new takeaway ditches. Water gushed into my pool within half an hour of a sudden storm. An hour after that, the input had ceased.

The obvious conclusion was that genuinely natural drainage allowed rainfall to soak the earth like a sponge. Only when it was sodden, and the water conserved, did the overspill trickle away down the ditch. So I blamed the unnaturally low level of our pool onto the scientifically efficient drainage of my neighbour, who had caused it to gush off towards the sea and be wasted instead of being naturally conserved.

The author at Chatsworth in Derbyshire

It is so low this year, even after the recent rains, that I can walk to the island without it going over the top of my rubber boots.

The first thing that struck me, when I got to Chatsworth, was how much greener the grass in the Park there is. This is not because it is soused in artificial fertiliser, as modern whizz-kid farmers do, because the Duke and Duchess of Devonshire object to chemical pesticides and other excessively intensive methods and prefer to see grass grazed and fertilised naturally, by sheep and cattle.

Before I'd worked there for a week, it had become crystal clear that the ground there was well watered! One minute the sun was shining as bright as on the Riviera, the next, black clouds had rolled from nowhere and it was bucketting down with rain. Height might have something to do with it, but not much. Our wood is 500 feet above the sea and Chatsworth is about twice that. But I wouldn't expect

500 feet to make the difference there obviously is in the weather there.

The secret, I suppose, is more concerned with the surrounding hills, which cause eddies and funnels of wind, and wring out the clouds like a sponge.

One day the River Derwent, which runs along the foot of the park, was gentle and well behaved, the water flowing over the weir as a disciplined curtain of water. The heavens opened that night, and when I returned, an angry torrent of swirling froth, as brown as Windsor soup, threatened death and destruction to anyone foolhardy enough to challenge it.

The Duke of Devonshire, who was also watching the sheep dog trials, appeared utterly oblivious to weather. He said he despised overcoats and that he could change his jacket when he got home, if it was thoroughly soaked. His grandmother had told him that if he was going to live at Chatsworth he'd better get used to rain – and it certainly appeared to have done him no harm.

His whole rolling parkland was brilliantly green and fertile, but well enough sloped to be effectively drained. Our ground is heavy clay, which holds what water we get – but I think I'd be prepared to learn to despise coats for rainfall enough to supply such brilliantly green fertility.

64. *Sylvan Free-for-all*

This time last year, the prophets of disaster were whinging about the imminent extinction of oak trees, which they predicted were bound to follow the English elms into oblivion. They based their forecast on the fact that there were very few acorns last year. They gave as their reason the theory that acorns were subject to some unnamed foreign disease, imported with foreign timber as Dutch elm disease had been.

I am delighted to report that they were wrong. I have rarely seen a better crop in our wood. I reckon that last year's poor crop was simply because the trees were taking a normal rest, as they do after years of bounty. The most obvious result of our bumper acorn harvest is that the deer seem to have taken leave of their senses. Instead of lying-up in deep cover most of the hours between dawn and dusk, they spend hours wandering aimlessly. Every few yards, they stop in their tracks and listen, as if they are haunted by some spook at the back of their minds. Then they change direction, dart into the wood and nuzzle the undergrowth, almost as if they wanted to hide their heads. The explanation is far less romantic. They stop in their tracks because they are listening not for spooks but for the sound of falling acorns. They change direction and make a dash for the source of the sound simply because their greed drives them to eat the fallen berry before their fellows find it.

An astonishing number of wild creatures love acorns. Pheasants will travel miles for them and they seem to know by instinct where oak woods in their territory are. Squirrels love them, as everybody knows, and they seem to drop as many as they eat, besides burying a few as insurance against winter hunger. This is probably wasted effort, because it is very doubtful if they remember where they hid them. Many sprout and come up the following year as infant oak trees.

Great flocks of rooks are congregating in the tops of our oaks,

Typical English hardwood

squabbling and jostling noisily to feast faster than their fellows. In the process, a large percentage of their plunder falls, uneaten, to the ground, for the deer to gorge upon. I am especially fond of the rooks because we had a rookery in the great lime trees by the back door of our last house. Their noisy courtship used to wake us at first light so that we could lie in bed and watch the pranks they played upon each other. Their nests are untidy mounds of twigs, gathered with great labour from far and wide. I have often visualised the task of persuading a random bundle of twigs to knit together in a nest strong enough to cradle a clutch of eggs safe against the wildest spring tempest.

What must have been infuriating was that just as one pair had almost completed their nest and were having to range farther afield to collect the exact twigs they wanted to finish it off, their neighbours moved in and pulled their nest apart in their absence. They took the easy twigs from the nest next door instead of getting stuck into the task of collecting their own.

At this time of the year, rook relationships are better. There are plenty of acorns for all. Meanwhile, the deer have cashed in to guzzle the surplus the rooks and squirrels have spilled. Although they heard the berries fall, some fell among thick grass and bilberry plants or bracken which completely hid the banquet from view. The deer froze in their tracks and, through my powerful binoculars, I could see their noses twitch, questing the air for clues of scent. Then they closed in on their prize, as unerringly as a pointer locates game, hidden in the undergrowth, for his master.

The crunch of the crumpling shells gave testimony that nothing is wasted by wildlife.

65. A Ray of Hope for Badgers*

The announcement in October 1984 of a report by the Dunnet Review Group, which was belatedly appointed by the Ministry of Agriculture to review the Ministry's badger extermination campaign, can be nothing but good news for badgers. Their whole campaign has been based on purely circumstantial evidence derived from laboratory experiments where healthy badgers were inoculated with massive doses of TB and kept in a cattle yard with calves, which ate off the floor where the badgers excreted. Even under these conditions it took up to six months for the calves to be infected. Such close contact under natural conditions in the wild is most unlikely.

It is therefore not surprising that knowledgeable countrymen were sceptical about the validity of the evidence on which the badgers were condemned to death. Doubt escalated to anger when the ministry rat-catchers gave a demonstration of how to catch badgers by using self-locking wire snares (which have since been made illegal on grounds of cruelty).

Fred Peart, the Minister at the time, was prosecuted for cruel ill treatment of a lactating sow badger, whose udder was split open by the steel wire, and although acquitted, he had costs awarded against him.

The Ministry then began gassing setts with potassium cyanide without even taking the elementary precaution of checking that their method was humane. In spite of continued public revulsion, it took seven years for them to admit that gassing was grossly inhumane and that it took the victims up to twenty-five minutes to die in agony.

By this time, public opposition was so fierce that Peter Walker, the Minister, was forced to call for an independent report, so he appointed Lord Zuckerman, an ageing scientist, to conduct it. Although many regarded the result as a whitewash, one constructive recommendation emerged. In October 1980 Zuckerman called for an independent

173

* This article was originally published in October 1984.

Badger digging has been illegal since 1973, but an effective defence against conviction was to claim the diggers 'thought it was a fox'. The law was strengthened in 1985 by an amendment to the Wildlife and Countryside Act which placed the onus on the diggers to prove they were not digging for badgers.

Some badgers are still dug illegally and sold to badger baiters who set dog after dog to attack them, 'reviving' them with sticks and stones when the badgers are overcome with wounds and weakness. The obscene 'sport' is as cruel to dogs as to badgers, and prizes are awarded for the most battle-scarred terrier.

This picture shows badger baiting in Ireland. The dog grips the badger's neck and is about to throttle it.

review in three years. The review team was announced, a year late, at the end of last September. It consists of Professor Dunnet, an ecologist, in the chair; Professor McInerny, an agricultural economist; and a vet from the London Zoo.

Yesterday, a ray of hope shone through. An organisation called Wildlife Link, under the auspices of the World Wildlife Fund UK, has been formed which includes the most highly respected conservation bodies in the country, under the chairmanship of Lord Melchett. ·It includes representatives of the British Association of Nature Conservationists, Fauna and Flora Preservation Society, Friends of the Earth, International Fund for Animal Welfare, Mammal Society, People's Trust for Endangered Species, Royal Society for Nature Conservation, RSPCA and World Wildlife Fund UK. It is such a formidable array of responsible and respectable conservationists that even the Ministry of Agriculture will ignore them at their peril.

The report is restrained, but detailed, running to 111 pages, and highly scientific. It is also highly critical of the muddle the Ministry has made.

Experience since the badger extermination policy began in 1975 has demonstrated that reasoned arguments do not even dent the Ministry determination to go ahead, right or wrong. Nothing but determined, potentially vote-losing campaigns has had the least effect in limiting, but not stopping, snaring, and ending the disgraceful badger-gassing campaign.

The method used now, in addition to snaring, is catching alive in cage traps. In theory the victims are shot humanely, but in practice many are taken away live for experiments in the laboratory.

It took great public pressure to make trappers release lactating sow badgers, to prevent orphaned cubs being left to starve.

But supervision has been so lax that 108 traps have been stolen and it is believed that some are being used to catch live badgers for the 'sport' of badger-baiting with dogs.

I hope that the Wildlife Link team will provide the best of both worlds, forcing the Ministry to take constructive instead of destructive action, by the logic of their arguments, and mustering public opposition if they refuse to see reason and exercise compassion.

66. *Feast of Voles*

Birds are not the only visitors to our bird-table. We put out very little food during the spring and summer because, being as lazy as sloppy housewives, birds tend to take easy options and feed their young on any unsuitable food – provided it is convenient. By leaving the bird-table bare, we force them to nourish their fledglings on natural food, even though they have to work hard to get it.

Now winter is approaching, I have hung hunks of fat from the branches of the tree in front of my study window and put corn and bruised apples on the bird-table. Tits and a solitary nut-hatch are feasting on the fat, blackbirds and thrushes on the apples and a motley array of sparrows and finches on the corn.

Later on, when times are harder, the deer will queue for the corn and apples, but the whole woodland floor is covered with acorns which the deer like so much that they gorge until they can hardly waddle to the bird-table.

The birds waste more than they can eat and spill skitherings of wheat upon the ground, which the woodmice and voles are very quick to exploit.

Light from the sitting-room window floods out on to the bird-table and illuminates the ground below.

Within days of laying out the feast, a bank vole had taken lodgings in a hollow of the haha wall, which stops the deer jumping on to the lawn to raid the garden. He was soon joined by another and another, until there was quite a colony of them feeding on the crumbs that fell from food wasted by the birds above.

Voles are pretty, chubby creatures and we derived great pleasure from watching them pick up a single grain of corn and twirl it delicately between their diminutive pink feet as they nibbled it away with yellow fangs that are anything but attractive. By last weekend, their

The wood mouse is a favourite prey of weasels

numbers were dwindling and shortage of food was certainly not the reason.

The cause turned out to be a weasel which had taken up residence in the rockery. We watched him, half hidden on the edge of the circle of light, stalking a fat and idle vole which had just about gorged himself to a standstill. The weasel, lithe and as sleek as a blonde's mink coat, did a reconnaissance as thorough as a soldier before battle. His disappearing act would have put conjurers to shame because he moved so fast that he gave the illusion of vanishing into the rocks when he really slid behind them. It was rather unnecessary with the voles because, when he dashed in to attack, he had caught one before it even got a whiff of danger.

The woodmice were far more of a challenge. Their long tails and well-muscled legs gave them the agility of kangaroos and their huge protruding eyes made them almost a match for the weasel. Almost but not quite. When he set his sights on some woodmice, the whole ritual was far more sophisticated. He started some yards away, cartwheeling along in an acrobatic display that would win medals at the Olympics. Instead of diving down the nearest hole, as prudent mice would do, the woodmice froze into immobility, literally hypnotised by the performance, and before it dawned on them that this was no entertainment, the weasel broke off his dance, dived on to the group and carried off a victim.

It was riveting to watch and the bonus was that weasels are not as nocturnal as mice and voles. 'Our' weasel emerges in daylight hours as well. We were sitting in the sun-room, having coffee for elevenses this morning, when he came out onto the lawn. A blackbird was foraging for worms, but when it spotted the weasel it screamed out its alarm call and dashed at its traditional enemy, in mock attack. The weasel dived for cover in the flower border – and the blackbird, emboldened by the retreat of its enemy, followed up its advantage.

This was where I came in, for I'd seen weasels and stoats deceive their prey by feigning retreat before. The next act in the drama would have seen the hunter leap from some unsuspected crevice in the foliage and silence the blackbird's screams of anger. So I stepped smartly on to the lawn and scared them both away. I expect the weasel was cross but the blackbird's song celebrated his survival.

67. Poison on the Land*

Public pressure has been concentrating against the use of agricultural pesticides and weedkillers for more than twenty years, but it has had depressingly little effect. It started in the 1950s, when thousands of wood pigeons and other birds were found dead in the fields after the new crop of corn had been sown. Foxes were the next victims, though it was thought, at first, that they had contracted some unknown disease with symptoms similar to jaundice. The real cause eventually turned out to be poisoning which resulted from eating dead and dying birds that had taken a fatal dose of corn doped with the chemical Aldrin.

'Useful' birds and animals and insects were annihilated indiscriminately with the 'target' pests, so that sparrow hawks and falcons paid a fatal price for eating birds that ate the farmers' wheat. They didn't always eat enough poison to kill them. They gradually accumulated a sub-lethal dose in their fat which rendered them infertile. Naturalists noticed an unusual number of nests where the birds sat on eggs which never hatched. When these eggs were examined, it was discovered that they had abnormally thin shells and, when the contents were analysed, traces of Aldrin and Dieldrin were found, which were the substances the boffins had brewed up to annihilate the insect pests.

The soil was so contaminated that the surplus water was also affected and swilled into ditches and brooks, killing fish, frogs and insects in the water. Otters and herons and kingfishers died from secondary poisoning when they ate the frogs.

Not surprisingly, responsible members of the public were so distressed by the carnage that there was a terrible outcry. Eventually three of the chlorinated hydrocarbon poisons were 'banned', though by agreement, not by law.

As some sort of sop to the public, the Ministry of Agriculture issues an annual booklet under the title of *Approved Products for Farmers and Growers*. Last year's edition ran to over 250 pages of chemicals listed

* This article was originally published in November 1984.

under the Agricultural Approval Scheme and a superficial examination might con the public that it is really what its title implies. Closer scrutiny soon dispels such optimism. An apparently innocuous brew called Vamidothion, for example, is prescribed for the control of aphids, red spider mites, sawfly and raspberry mite. A footnote, labelled 'Caution', advises farmers not to use it if they are under medical advice not to work with antichlorinesterase compounds, adding innocently that animals and poultry should be kept away from treated areas for four weeks! If that does not put your hackles up, have a look at the section under Drazoxolon fungicide. Livestock must be kept off treated areas for four weeks and it is dangerous to livestock and fish. Not the sort of stuff that I should like to lend my name to approve as a product for farmers and growers!

So, when the government announced recently that it was asking Parliament for approval for a bill to grant ministers sweeping powers to control pesticides, few jumped up and down with unqualified delight. Their 'approved' guide for farmers and growers has proved to be little more than a catalogue of death. It licences obscene chemicals to be spewed on the land to the detriment of wildlife for the sake of minimal additions to the surplus food mountains which plague our economy.

Recent deaths from salmonella poisoning are thought to be due to new strains of resistant salmonella in poultry and meat. This resistance has been caused by the increasing use of antibiotics in animal feed-stuffs to control disease resulting from overstocking. This 'doctoring' of feedstuffs with antibiotics and sex hormones can have horrific effects on the health and sex life of those who eat the meat and the fact that the Ministry of Agriculture has taken no voluntary steps to control them has done nothing for their credibility.

Fuel is added to this smouldering fire by the fact that the government refuses to publish draft regulations before the bill becomes law. It demands that Parliament shall approve the regulations, without seeing them, and must accept or reject them, without amendment. A more acceptable option would be that the Ministry of Agriculture be limited to making *recommendations*, while the Nature Conservancy Council, or some other responsible body, should be given the power to grant or refuse a licence.

68. Master Bucks' Music

Fallow deer most years keep almost to the calendar. They cast their antlers in May, have grown a new and even more glamorous set by August, and then they choose the best territory they can for a honeymoon.

There is as much jostling for the most desirable spots as there is between tycoons in industry. The strongest and most vigorous bucks pick clearings in the trees that will accommodate a large harem of desirable does. Then the bucks work themselves into a frenzy by thrashing overhanging branches to ribbons with their newly developed antlers and scraping hollows in the peaty woodland floor with their hooves. By the first or second week in October they have annexed their territory and are ready to welcome the most attractive females in the wood.

The way they set about it would not turn on fastidious lovers of good music. The best description of their love song is a bawdy belch, though charitable country folk say that they can hear the bucks 'groaning'. Female fallow deer appreciate it, though, and begin to accept the buck of their fancy as a prospective partner. Meanwhile, rival bucks groan back their challenges to the master buck – and invitations to his does.

The third week in October is usually the peak of activity in our wood, and if there happens to be a good early frost at the time, the rut is often a fiery affair with bucks sparring and groaning and chivvying the does into their territory. The night air is riven with martial sounds of threat and counter-threat, with occasional syncopation as angry antlers clash when bluff is called. The best and most active ruts are short-lived. The master bucks mate all the does which come into heat almost simultaneously and then drift away to find their own favourite feeding areas as soon as the honeymoon is over. Lesser bucks keep just out of harm's way, skulking round the edge of their superior

A fallow buck

rivals' harems, hoping to take over when the passion of their elders is spent.

This year has been exceptional because there has hardly been any music – if groaning can be so described. The master buck in our wood has a truly magnificent pair of antlers and he staked out his territory by the pool just across the paddock from the house. His love song was muted and half-hearted and about fifteen does seem to cluster round more in hope than expectation.

A smaller buck, a year younger, came and made rude gestures but it was obvious that his challenge was no more than bluff and the old man scarcely bothered to chivvy him off.

Honey, the white doe I reared on the bottle twelve years ago, has not forgotten what it is all about, for there is life in the old doe yet. She failed to have a fawn last year and we feared that she was feeling her age, but this year she's had the most delightful spotted beauty of her whole family. She's obviously determined to repeat the performance next summer! That is, if her spouse has more about him than it seems.

So instead of having the wood filled with music of hope for the future there was nothing much but muted groans that went on for weeks instead of days. When it faded into silence the only optimistic signs were that all the bucks had lost so much weight that they might have had some foul disease that had really run them down. This was because their one-track minds are concentrated so much on romance that even in such a slack year they didn't bother about their food.

Last year the acorn harvest was so bad that all the deer had for recuperation was flabby grass and leaves. This year there are more acorns than I have ever seen, and acorns are superb food for birds and beasts. The moment the rut was over, the bucks began to gorge on them, and within days their coats shone with health and they were as sleek as moles so that they filled my eyes with pleasure when they came into the sunlit clearings.

Romance sometimes flies out of the window with five-star menus because the way to a man's and deer's heart, it seems, is through his stomach, but some might think the bucks were overdoing it this year.

Index

italic folios indicate illustrations